the books of
II Timothy & Titus

Henry Vander Kam

Reformed Fellowship, Inc.
3363 Hickory Ridge Ct. SW
Grandville, MI 49418

©2007 Reformed Fellowship, Inc.
Printed in the United States of America.
All rights reserved

For information:
Reformed Fellowship, Inc.
3363 Hickory Ridge Ct. SW
Grandville, MI 49418
Phone: 616.532.8510
Web: reformedfellowship.net
Email: sales@reformedfellowship.net

Book design by Jeff Steenholdt

ISBN 0-9793677-0-0

Contents

Greetings and Encouragement *1*

Paul an Example for Timothy *7*

To Be a Minister in Such a Time as This *13*

The Stability of the Church *19*

The Work of a Pastor *25*

The Coming Times *31*

Encouragement in Difficulties *37*

The Scriptures *43*

Preach the Word *49*

Paul's Last Words *55*

Greetings and Purpose *63*

The Conditions at Crete *69*

The Christian Family *75*

Our Responsibility to the Gospel *81*

Attitude Toward Non-Christians *87*

Final Instructions and Greetings *93*

Lesson 1

Greetings and Encouragement

II Timothy 1:1-7

The second epistle to Timothy was written under quite different conditions than those which obtained while Paul was writing his first letter to Timothy. Paul is now in his second, and final, imprisonment. This second imprisonment was much more severe than the first. During his first imprisonment he was able to communicate with friends, was able to preach the gospel, and was even allowed to live in his own rented house.

Now all is different. Emperor Nero is harsh in his treatment of prisoners. Paul is fully aware of the fact that he is awaiting execution. Nero will show no mercy and his hatred of the Christians will insure the death of the greatest of Apostles.

Paul's concern

This epistle is the last Paul ever wrote. Understandably, it is written to Timothy, his son and successor. It is brief — there is little time to write. What does he write about? Does he write about his own sorry state as a prisoner and seek to elicit the sympathy of Timothy? Not at all. He is a true Apostle of Jesus Christ and the service of His Lord is his only concern.

The church, His body, is therefore Paul's concern. Dangerous times are coming for the church. He warns and counsels Timothy to arm the church with the truth of God. Sound doctrine alone will safeguard the church of Jesus Christ. That Paul is in prison and that death awaits him — these are matters which are under the control of his God.

He is willing to die for his Savior. But, the church must be protected and strengthened!

Salutation

The salutation at the beginning of this letter is very similar to the one at the beginning of Paul's first epistle to Timothy. This salutation makes it clear that this is not merely a personal letter, but that it is intended as revelation. It is a letter written by Apostolic authority.

Paul always magnifies his office. He is an Apostle of Christ Jesus, through the will of God. He has been *called* to a task. That *calling* gave him authority. Not because he *is doing the work* does he have office, but because his God has given him the calling to do it. Paul then speaks of the content of the message he was to bring. He is called to labor with and in the gospel which he here characterizes as the promise of the life which is in Christ Jesus. *That* is the gospel! John has often so characterized it. It is that fullness of life now, and such a complete and full life as is still to come.

Only the gospel gives true and full life. As in the first epistle, so now too Paul declares the grace, mercy, and peace of God upon Timothy. His address to Timothy is even more endearing than in the former epistle. He calls him "my beloved child."

Thanksgiving

Immediately Paul begins the letter proper. As he does so often, so here too he begins with thanksgiving. This is understandable in many of the other epistles, but he is now writing from prison and is staring death in the face. Yet, there is room for thanksgiving.

Paul is not cast down in spirit. He does not say specifically what he is thankful for, although the immediately following words seem to indicate that he is

Greetings and Encouragement

thankful for Timothy! He states that he has served God from his forefathers in a pure conscience. We know very little about Paul's early life. Evidently he was the product of a Godfearing home.

Paul's view of life and his beliefs were in agreement with the true faith in Israel from earliest times. It was not the faith in Jesus Christ, but the faith of Old Testament Israel. He served his God zealously and in a pure conscience. His conscience was clear when he imprisoned men and women who believed in Christ. He thought he was doing God's service.

Prayers for Timothy

Paul remembers Timothy in his prayers day and night. The prayers of this Apostle did much for the success and growth of the early church. He has a strong desire to see Timothy again. Whether or not this is possible, the writer does not say, but he hopes Timothy will be able to come before winter (4:12). Such a visit would fill him with joy. It would also be very profitable for Timothy.

Paul remembers the tears his spiritual son shed when last they parted. But, if there were tears when they parted the last time, it might be even worse when he sees Paul in his present condition. Despite that emotional difficulty, they ought to meet so that Paul may show him that there are more important things to consider than the death of this Apostle.

Timothy's faith

Paul has been reminded of the true and healthy faith of Timothy. This is the all-important thing. This is the faith which his grandmother professed, his mother embraced, and is also found in him. Although faith is not inherited, God nevertheless works covenantly — he works in families.

This is not the same faith of which Paul spoke in verse 3

in which he had served his God as his forefathers did. Paul's early faith was without the knowledge of Jesus Christ. Timothy had been brought up in the faith which is in Christ Jesus. He had never experienced that radical conversion such as Paul had experienced on the way to Damascus. He would not be able to say when or where he had been converted. Some believe that this lack of conversion experience impoverishes. Paul doesn't. It was a shame that Christ had to intervene violently in his life. He had been going in the wrong direction, which made this conversion experience necessary. Timothy, on the other hand, had served Jehovah from his youth! That is beautiful!

Instructions for Timothy

Hopefully Paul and Timothy will be able to meet, and when they do, there will be much personal profit for both. However, the Apostle is writing this epistle as the one who has been charged with all the needs of the church and as the vehicle of revelation. Their personal needs and desires are not to be foremost, but the affairs of the church will have the most prominent place on the agenda.

Nor can these affairs of the church wait until the two may meet again. Very gently, but also very firmly, Paul tells Timothy how he is to conduct himself. He has so many fine qualities! However, he also has various weaknesses. If these weaknesses are allowed to dominate, the church will suffer. From the first epistle it is clear that Timothy labored under various difficulties. He is not another Paul! He is timid by nature, and the troubles and persecutions which are about to come upon the church will not be overcome by timidity. He is relatively young, and the enemies of the cross are veteran warriors. He has a weak physique, and the affairs of the church will demand day and night work in the times to come. How will he ever be able to do the work assigned to him, and then, with Paul no longer on the scene?

Greetings and Encouragement

Paul now reminds Timothy that his strength is not to be sought in himself. Nor is strength to be sought in his mother. Then he would have to conclude that Paul was indispensable. The Apostle has never had that exalted view of his own importance. Christ, who is on the throne and ruling all the affairs of men, has decided to remove Paul from this earthly scene. He does all things well. Paul not only submits to this divine ruling, he is agreeable to it! Timothy may not go contrary to the divine will. Surely, there have been tears, and that is understandable. But, this may not continue! There is work to be done and *the church is much more important than any one person!*

Gently and firmly Paul tells Timothy that he must stir up the gift of God which is in him. He has the true faith, handed down from grandmother and mother. Paul has laid his hands on him to symbolize the reception of the Holy Spirit and office. The gift of God is therefore present. He must not act as though he has not received it. Nor may he neglect that gift. He has a responsibility towards it. That gift was given him for a purpose — to feed and tend the church of Jesus Christ. Come on now! Stir up that gift! It must be fanned into a brightly burning flame! Don't dwell constantly on the sadness of the circumstances and your own inadequacies, but lay hold on the power which has been given you which is able to do the work to which you are called.

The gift which God has given is not a spirit of fearfulness. Timothy has such a fearful spirit. That was not God's doing. That was his own. He must take hold of himself to rid himself of his fears. He may not excuse himself by saying: that is the way I am. Every believer must realize that his faith must change his personality too. No, God gave him the spirit of power! That power he needs and he wishes that he had more power. Well, he has it — he only needs to stir it up. In that power of the Spirit he will be able to accomplish all his Savior has given him to do. The work is God's and He can use any vessel He chooses.

The spirit of power which God gives is never a raw power. It is also a spirit of love. He alone is able to combine these two forces and both are necessary in the work Timothy will have to do. Unlimited power combined with a most tender love! What a combination! He is able to do it, being Almighty God; and willing to do it, being a gracious Father! Besides, the gift which the Spirit of God bestows includes self-discipline. If Timothy stirs up the gift which has been given him, he will have the mastery over himself.

Questions for discussion:
1. What was the effect of Nero's persecution on the growth of the church?
2. What determines office — the calling or the work? Or both?
3. Do you wish you could state the hour of your conversion? Why not? Do we not often consider those to be heroes who were brought out of the gutter to faith in Christ?
4. We often say that everything must come under the influence of the gospel. Are our own personalities often the last to come under its influence?
5. Of what significance was the laying on of hands?

Lesson 2

Paul an Example for Timothy

II Timothy 1:8-18

Although Paul does not refer to himself or his condition to stir up a feeling of pity in the heart of Timothy, he is not afraid to call attention to himself as an example to be followed. This characteristic is in all of his writings. This does not reveal a spirit of pride, but of complete honesty. He is so thoroughly convinced of the genuineness of his beliefs and the life-style which flows from it that he calls others to imitate him.

Not ashamed of the gospel

Paul counsels Timothy not to be ashamed of the gospel of Jesus Christ. This is a rather negative approach but it will bring the various problems Timothy and others may have into clear focus.

Look where that gospel has led! That gospel has been foolishness to the Greeks; and are they not being confirmed in their views? The greatest of all who have followed this gospel is now a prisoner in a miserable dungeon in Rome. Don't be ashamed of me either, continues Paul. Be sure to see these things in the proper perspective. I am not Nero's prisoner, first of all, but the prisoner of Jesus Christ! He has regulated all things in such a way as to make me a prisoner and halt my usual work. He is still in control.

Suffer hardship

Instead of being ashamed of the gospel and of the Apostle of Christ, Timothy should be ready to suffer the persecutions which attend the gospel. The power of God will enable him to do it. The gospel is worth it. Despite hardship, persecution, and imprisonment, Christ saved us!

We are saved in spite of outward appearances. Paul refers to the complete salvation through the blood of our Lord. He called us to service. No, not because of our own innate goodness, for this we did not have. He chose us for our tasks according to His own wise purpose — and in His grace. He fulfills His purposes and shows His grace in Christ Jesus.

This plan of God is not of recent date, no, it is a plan which was already framed before time began. Whenever Paul speaks of the salvation of His people and of the all-wise plan of God in His dealing with His people, he goes back before the world was. The election of God is the fountain out of which the present happenings flow. This election of God is always placed in the framework of grace. Election is not the "horrible doctrine," as some have thought, but it is the root out of which the stream of grace flows. If He has not chosen me — I would never have chosen Him!

Consider the "mysteries" made manifest — The results of God's work in eternity are now brought to light with the coming of Jesus Christ in the flesh. So often Paul speaks of the "mysteries" which were hidden before but are now made manifest. Such is also the thought here.

The saints of the Old Testament had true faith and an assured hope, but things were not yet clear — they were dwelling in shadows. With the first coming of Christ the sun has risen and the full light shines. Christ has abolished death, i.e., made it of none effect. These words come from the lips of one who is awaiting death by execution at the hand of Nero!

Really, says Paul, death isn't death anymore. Nero will be able to kill the body, but that isn't death. When Paul's body is slain he will be ushered into the very presence of his

Paul an Example for Timothy

Savior where a fullness of life will be his as he has never experienced before. To be with Him is far better. He has abolished eternal death and has brought life and immortality to light.

This radical change in the lives of men is brought to light in the gospel. No one else has ever come with a teaching or a philosophy which has such power. Now, of that gospel Paul had been appointed a preacher, and an Apostle, and a teacher. What higher position or honor can come to any man? Paul always stands in awe of that grace of God which appointed him to his life's work! To me, unworthy, persecutor, chief of sinners, was that grace given to make known the riches of God's grace and the will of God concerning their redemption! It should cause every minister of the gospel to quake!

It is because of that gospel that Paul is now in chains, he realizes it. But, the gospel is worth it. He has urged Timothy not to be ashamed of that gospel. Timothy is still free. What the future holds for him is, of course, not known. However, he may also have to suffer for it in the days to come.

He should now look at the example of Paul. The Apostle is already suffering greatly; yet, he is not ashamed of the gospel. Regardless where it has brought him, he holds to the gospel and testifies to its adequacy whenever he can.

Rely on Christ

The reason for Paul's perfect confidence is now stated in words which have become very familiar to the Christian church in a very popular hymn. He knows whom he has believed. This is not a knowledge of acquaintance, but far more. The One whom he has learned to know is the God who has never put him to shame and the Savior in whom he has everything.

There is simply nothing which can obscure Paul's view of Christ. He has committed something to Him. Several times in the pastoral epistles he speaks of something which has been entrusted to either Timothy or himself. Here he speaks of something which he has entrusted to His Savior.

He does not say what it is. It is, however, clear that it is the most important thing for him. It is so-important that he will suffer all the pain and indignity of the present.

Paul has entrusted himself and his eternal salvation — all his hopes — into the hands of Christ. He has the confidence that Christ will guard this for him. It would not be safe even in his own hands. Persecution might then shake it loose. However, Christ will keep it safely for him until the day he appears before Him to claim it. This is the kind of trust which cannot be placed in any other. Our faith and hope are to be anchored in Jesus Christ.

Hold the pattern of sound works

On the basis of the foregoing he now counsels Timothy to follow his example again. He must hold "the pattern of sound words" which he has been taught by the Apostle. By this he means the true doctrine which will give the confidence that he possesses. One has to know the truth well to be able to have no fears when execution for the sake of the gospel is approaching. Then you cannot "get by" with only a very shallow acquaintance with the gospel. It is brought to the test!

That gospel is able to give strength according to need, but only when there is a thorough knowledge of it. Time and again Paul stresses the importance of sound doctrine. How is it possible that there are still many today who minimize the importance of it! Not only is it necessary for a strong personal faith to be able to stand in the day of persecution, but it is also an absolute necessity for the building up of the church. Timothy has been taught the true doctrine by Paul. Paul was not satisfied with skimming the surface. He gave, not only to Timothy and Titus, but also the churches, a strong diet!

Paul an Example for Timothy

That good thing, the gospel, guard! Don't let anyone take it away from you, but let no one dilute it either. *That* is the greatest danger. Many have kept a "skeleton" gospel. Then there is no life or power. Let us realize that it can only be kept through the Holy Spirit.

Disloyalty and loyalty

The Apostle concludes this moving chapter with a reference to his own state at the present time. Although he certainly does not refer to these things to stir to pity, the entire epistle is written against the background of his imprisonment.

Paul now mentions the fact that he has been disappointed in fellow believers. All those of Asia have turned away from him. There was the possibility in the Roman system that friends of the accused might come forward in his defense. However, this was not without danger. There was always the distinct possibility of being charged with the same crimes as the prisoner. The believers of Asia considered the danger to be too great. No doubt they loved Paul and had, perhaps, been converted under his ministry. However, to love someone or to put your life or liberty in jeopardy, are two different things. They did not have the confidence which Paul had. Two of these are mentioned by name although we do not know who they were.

On the other hand, Paul was refreshed by the coming of Onesiphorus. This man was not ashamed "of my chain" and was not fearful for his own safety. When he came to Rome he looked for Paul and found him. Many questions have been raised concerning these two verses. Did he have to look for him? The fact that Paul hopes that mercy may be granted to "the house of Onesiphorus" raises the question in the minds of some whether he might have died before Timothy receives this letter. Such questions are fruitless because there are no answers — only speculation.

Paul says that Onesiphorus proved to be a dedicated disciple. He ran risks for the sake of Paul the prisoner. May God reward him at the last day for the good deeds he has done and may that reward also be extended to his household.

Some, though believers, do not possess that Christian heroism which may be required. The Apostle Peter didn't have it the night Jesus Christ was tried. Others, such as Daniel and Onesiphorus, do have that heroism. Why the difference? Cling to the sound words — that only makes heroes!

Questions for discussion:
1. How important is the doctrine of election? If you did not believe in election would you have any assurance for the future?
2. Could we have chosen for God if He had not chosen us? What do you think of the question: Won't you accept Christ?
3. Which is the more important — doctrine or life? Or is this a faulty contrast?
4. What makes a person heroic in the time of trial? Can you tell whether or not you would be heroic at that time before that time arrives?

Lesson 3

To be a Minister in Such a Time as This

II Timothy 2:1-13

In contrast to those who have forsaken him in the hour of his greatest need and in keeping with the attitude of Onesiphorus, Paul now urges Timothy to strengthen himself in the grace which is in Christ Jesus so that he may be able to do his work properly. His natural fearfulness must be overcome if he is to do the work of the ministry in the coming days.

The gifts Timothy has received are sufficient to qualify him to his task. Let him now lay hold on these gifts for his own welfare and for the welfare of the church he is called to serve. No doubt, the times will be difficult. However, he can draw on the grace of his Savior which will be sufficient regardless of circumstances.

A straight line of teaching

First of all, let it be clear that the church of Christ will go on and no circumstances can stop it. Nor does Timothy have to do the work alone. He must transmit the wealth of instruction he has received from Paul to others, faithful men, who in turn must instruct another group. So the church will go on.

Timothy has been in the presence of Paul so much in the past and has, together with many other witnesses, heard Paul expound the depths of the gospel of Jesus Christ. These truths he must now commit to others. These are the sound, the "healthy" words, the true doctrine, which must be taught. Let there be a straight line of teaching from the Apostle to Timothy to faithful men to others. Thus the church will grow and the truth of the gospel will be guarded.

Called as a soldier

This teaching, however, will not be accomplished in the atmosphere of the quiet scholarly life or out of ivory towers. No, in this time it will have to be accomplished amid grave personal dangers. Paul holds this realistic picture clearly before his beloved child. Timothy should realize that he too has been called as a soldier of Jesus Christ. Although his personality longs to be "carried to the skies on flowery beds of ease," that is not to be expected in the days in which he is called to minister to the church. He will be called to suffer as many others also have. He must show himself to be a good soldier of Christ Jesus. A soldier in battle lives in the midst of grave danger every moment and might lose his life.

How must Timothy (and, in a wider sense, all ministers) conduct himself in his ministry? Paul uses three illustrations to make this clear. First of all, he likens the work of the ministry to that of a soldier. A soldier must be a *soldier* all the time! He must not have interests on the side which detract from his main calling. He may not be engaged in the business of the world for his personal profit. His calling as a soldier demands *full time!* He has to carry out the orders of his superior. Only in that way will he be able to please him "who enrolled him as a soldier." While a soldier is "on service" he may not ask for an eight-hour day! He may have to work the full twenty-four hours. So must Timothy, and all those who follow him in his calling, recognize his commitment.

Contending in a game

The next illustration the Apostle uses is taken from the

world of sports. The purpose is to win, to be crowned. He uses this figure frequently and often speaks of the training and discipline which is required. Yet, the goal is to win. No one is eligible to win if he does not abide by the rules of the particular game in which he was contending. So must Timothy, and those who follow him, contend according to the rules.

The ministry too has rules. Only the true gospel, the Word of God, may be brought. All other teaching is contraband. Beautiful poetry, philosophy, or the news of the day may never take the place of the gospel! It is unlawful, and what is unlawful is sin.

Like a farmer

The third illustration which is used is from the area of farming. The farmer who works diligently for a whole season must be the first to partake of the fruits of his labors. This is the only fair method. He has earned this reward. So too with a minister. He is called upon to suffer in times of stress, he has to work long and hard to prepare the harvest, he may then also rejoice in the firstfruits of the harvest. While the season lasts there may be various disappointments. He will have to work long and hard, but the work brings its own rewards. Paul is now suffering for the gospel, but he has also had rich rewards for his labors.

The illustrations which Paul has used must not be taken lightly. There is always the danger that the illustration will be remembered but the matter it illustrates forgotten. He therefore urges Timothy to consider carefully the things he has taught by means of these illustrations. They will reveal to him the essence of the gospel ministry. These teachings he needs. He may not be able to assimilate all of that which the Apostle has taught him in these three verses at once, but, if he considers, ponders, these matters, the Lord will give him understanding in all things.

Look to the risen Christ

Although Timothy must be prepared to suffer many things for the sake of the gospel, he should not be unduly depressed by this fact. He should always keep his eye directed to Jesus Christ risen from the dead. The fact that Jesus, Who also suffered more than any other, is risen from the dead is the indication that He lives forever. He is of the seed of David, the true King whose kingdom has no end.

That Christ, risen from the dead and seated on the throne of the universe, must always stand out clearly in your mind. Then the direction of your life will be straight and you will not be led astray by present circumstances and difficulties.

Suffering hardship

That gospel Paul had proclaimed; and for the proclamation of that gospel he was now suffering hardship unto bonds. Yet, he tells Timothy to do the same thing, and, of course, it may have the same results.

Paul is considered to be a malefactor, a criminal. Those who uphold the law of God and the laws of men are now considered criminals! But the gospel is not bound! You instruct faithful men, and let them again instruct others in that gospel! Preach it to all men! The gospel is not in chains! This fact gives the Apostle the courage to endure all things for the sake of those whom God has chosen to faith and obedience. They will obtain the salvation which is in Christ Jesus with eternal glory.

The question, however, arises: How does Paul's endurance of his sufferings work for the salvation of others at a later date? One answer is that he knows the gospel will be victorious in spite of the fact that he was made non-active through his imprisonment.

Yet, there seems to be further reason. Humanly speaking, if Paul had not given the right answer to his tormentors, the faith of many would have been shaken. The eyes of the church are on him as he stands before his accusers. As Christ gave the good confession before Pontius Pilate, so Paul gave the good confession before Nero. The leader must recognize his responsibility to those he leads!

A faithful saying

At the conclusion of this section the Apostle again, as he does several times in the Pastoral Epistles, refers to that which has become a faithful saying. It is a confession generally accepted — perhaps in the form of a stanza of a hymn.

The words of this "saying" are now applied to Timothy in his work as a minister in these times. This "stanza" consists of several lines following the same pattern. It is: If we do this — Christ will do that. They are statements so obviously true, no one is expected to deny them. If we died with Him we shall also live with Him. Remember, this is to be applied to Timothy. Even though the martyr's lot awaits, that is not the end, for we shall live with Him who is risen from the dead. Fear not them which are able to kill the body! Should you have to die as a martyr for the sake of the gospel, you will be ushered into the full life with Jesus! This truth Paul has applied to himself!

"If we endure (that is, the suffering of the present time), we shall also reign with him." He who endures till the end shall be saved. "If we deny him, he also will deny us." Those who confess Him, He will confess before His father and before the angels; but, the contrary is also true. The last line of this "stanza" has given some difficulty. Some think it means: Whether we are faithful or not, He is always faithful because He cannot deny Himself. However, this goes contrary to the whole train of thought expressed in this faithful saying. In complete harmony with the foregoing it means: If we are faithless in respect to the gospel, He is faithful to His own threats in regard to this. He will not

II Timothy & Titus

condone unfaithfulness. He would have to deny His own being to overlook this. *That* he cannot do — He cannot deny Himself! He will "reward" faithlessness according to its desserts.

The times are difficult. Nevertheless, Timothy must be a true servant of Jesus Christ. All the things necessary for the true ministry are at his disposal. Christ will guard His church and cause it to grow.

Questions for discussion:
1. How can we strengthen ourselves in faith?
2. Which are some of the dangers peculiar to the ministry? Don't we usually think that a minister's faith is the strongest?
3. Paul made tents. Was this contrary to what he tells Timothy — that he should give full-time to the gospel ministry?
4. The gospel is old. Many people would like to hear new things. Does the gospel also satisfy the craving of these people? May ministers give in to the desire to have something "different"?
5. What are some of the firstfruits of which a minister partakes?
6. Does a minister's heresy affect himself only? Explain.

Lesson 4

The Stability of the Church

II Timothy 2:14-19

In the pastoral epistles Paul deals essentially with the welfare of the church for the future and the role the offices play in the welfare of the church. Timothy is Paul's immediate successor and he must see to it that there will be others to stand at his side and to continue the work after he too must relinquish the reins.

Paul has written concerning these matters to Timothy but he must see to it that the other officebearers will be instructed in these same things. The things of which he has written in the previous paragraph are of great importance to everyone who is charged with the oversight of the church of Christ. They must all teach the same thing and they must all have the same attitude to office.

Dangerous teachings

In the first epistle Paul had spoken of various teachers who led the people astray. He now refers to the same teachers. Evidently things still have not improved regarding this matter. In the former epistle he had characterized these teachings as myths and old wives' fables.

Such teachers would go on endlessly about genealogies, etc. It was essentially a striving about words. This is of no profit — useless. With this kind of teaching they obscure the gospel of Jesus Christ. Then it becomes dangerous — not an innocent exercise. They are undermining the faith of the people. Instead of giving them the true food for their spiritual life, they "feed" them with that which is of no profit. Timothy must make an end to this practice. He must charge them in the sight of the Lord! It must be made plain to these so-called teachers that the Lord of the church condemns their practice.

A workman approved by God

How should the true servant of God conduct himself? The true servants of God must live in the realization that he is accountable to his God! God will be the Judge of his work. Men-pleasers will never pass the test. Therefore His servants must do their utmost to receive divine approval. This will produce various difficulties because the approval of God and the approval of men are not always the same.

This fact had brought many sufferings into Paul's life. Yet, God's approval is the only one that counts, in the final analysis. Timothy must therefore see to it that he receives divine approval both in the present time and in the moment he stands before God's throne.

That divine approval will be given him if he is a conscientious workman. The amount of work to be done is staggering. He must be a *workman* rather than a *striver* about words. As a *workman* he will do the tasks assigned. The work he is called to do will be so great and so arduous that it may well consume him. How can anyone have the impression that the work of a minister of the gospel is easy? It will be work for both day and night — if he takes the word of God and the importance of the church seriously. His conscience must be clear, he may not be ashamed of the quality of the work he performs. If one does not do his best he will be ashamed before the people of God; and, what is more important, before God Himself. Let His servants labor in such a way that the divine approval may rest on both them and their work.

Proclaim the Word

The most important work to which God's servants are

The Stability of the Church

called is the proclamation of the Word. The servant of God must handle aright the Word of truth. Great care must be taken in the use of this Word because the church must be fed by it. The God of truth does not want His words to be twisted.

If the church does not receive the true Word from its ministers its growth will be stunted and its health impaired. That Word of truth is the revelation of the mind of God and is, therefore, often difficult to understand by the mind of man. To handle that Word aright is a tremendous task!

Let the servant of God agonize over that Word until he is able to handle it properly! There is too much at stake to take this task lightly. The manner in which His servants handle the Word of truth will determine the spiritual health or sickness of the members of the church for years to come.

Shun profane babblings

To show how important it is that the Word of truth be handled properly, the Apostle again refers to the unfaithful teachers at Ephesus. Timothy must not allow himself to be detracted from his own labors by them. Shun these profane babblings! Don't debate them. Ignore them! They will go on to further ungodliness. That which may have seemed to be innocent speculation to some will go from bad to worse.

Whenever the Word of God is used in the manner in which these "teachers" use it, it can do nothing but increase in ungodliness. The one error leads to the other. Therefore one must be so careful in the handling of God's Word. The teachings of these men will eat like a gangrene. It will destroy healthy tissue and spread farther and farther. It is deadly! Its progress is often far greater than the victim realizes. When it is recognized — it is too late.

Heretics renounced

Paul is not merely mentioning an unidentified group, he

also becomes very specific. Let the heretics be mentioned by name so that everyone may be on his guard. He mentions Hymenaeus, who had also been mentioned in the first chapter of the first epistle, and Philetus, who is named for the first time. We do not know anything about these individuals except that which the writer now says about them. No doubt, they were leaders among the false teachers and well known to Timothy.

Paul does not say that he disagrees with these men, but, much stronger, they have erred concerning the truth. They are heretics! They have wrested the Word of God! They teach that the resurrection is past! No future *resurrection of the body* is to be expected. Do they believe in a resurrection? Certainly and thereby they overthrow the faith of some. They use the same terminology as the true church does and pour an entirely different content into the terms they use. The resurrection — that was the rebirth! You arose from the state of sin to salvation! Now, doesn't that sound a deep spiritual note? The body isn't so important. The soul is the all-important thing.

Almost every heresy receives a hearing and this one is no exception. The faith of some has been turned upside down. This type of teaching is a mixture of the gospel and Greek philosophy. The seat of evil, according to some of the Greeks, is in the body. To deny its resurrection might be applauded by some. However, Paul bases his whole gospel on the truth of the resurrection of the body! If Christ is not raised, then… They also minimize sin by stating that the real resurrection was our rebirth. What is then our present condition? Are we now perfect seeing we have already partaken of the resurrection? Indeed, our rebirth was a miracle of God's grace, but it was not the resurrection of which Scripture speaks.

The church stands

What is now the state of the church and what may be

The Stability of the Church

expected of the future? There are so many who are undermining the faith of His people. How shall that church stand under these conditions with no outlook for improvement on this score in the future? One would almost become despondent.

The Apostle, however, ends on an entirely different note. Regardless of all the difficulties both within and without, the firm foundation of God standeth! There has been much discussion about the question: what does he mean by this foundation? This is, I believe rather fruitless.

The context makes it very clear that Paul means the church. Indeed, at other times he refers to other things as foundations — but here it is clearly the church. In spite of all the opposition — the church stands. In spite of the attacks of Satan — the church stands. In spite of all unfaithful ministers — the church stands. It is the foundation which God has laid, therefore nothing is able to overthrow it. The gates of hell shall not prevail against it. This stability of the church is of the greatest comfort for those who belong to it. It is God's work and His work never fails.

There are many passages in the Pauline epistles where the author goes into the meaning and character of the church much more than he does in this particular place. However, the solidity and lasting character of the church is taught as strongly here as any other place. Timothy needs this. The times are difficult and will become worse but his labor is not in vain!

A seal with two sides

There is a seal on this foundation. This sounds rather strange, but the truth which the Apostle teaches is usually too rich to be contained in any one metaphor.

Seals are usually not found on foundations! This is a double seal — or one with two sides. On the one side is written: The Lord knoweth them that are his; and on the other: Let every one that nameth the name of the Lord depart from unrighteousness. The very fact that it is sealed reveals ownership and authenticity. Let no one break that seal!

By the first inscription God reveals that the church finds its origin in His election. He has chosen and purchased them so that the church is His property. The second inscription shows that certain requirements are made of those who form His church. They must be pure. Here His election and the responsibilities of the elect are brought together. They always belong together — no one may separate them even though no one can harmonize them.

Questions for Discussion:
1. Does topical preaching do justice to the Word of God? Explain.
2. How must the Word of God be handled or "divided?" Of what importance is the knowledge of the original languages in "handling" the word aright?
3. When different ministers or theologians use such terms as "Word of God," "election," "rebirth," etc., do they necessarily mean the same thing? How necessary is it to define the terms?
4. What is modernism's view of the resurrection?
5. Do we have any guarantee that "our church" will always remain?

Lesson 5

The Work of a Pastor

II Timothy 2:20-26

The work of a pastor is, of course, determined to a great extent by the calling of his Lord to preach the Word. Yet, the work is not the same for every pastor. His work will also be determined by the character of the people to whom he must minister and by times and conditions.

Although the needs of people are quite similar in every age, local conditions may demand specialized qualifications. Every minister realizes that we are still in the militant church and that perfection has not yet been attained.

Difficulties

Paul calls Timothy's attention to some of the difficulties he will encounter and tells him how he is to deal with them. By a figure he makes clear to Timothy that there will be many different kinds of people in the church to which he will minister.

Paul likens the church to a large house. In such a house there will be, of necessity, many different articles so that the household will run smoothly. The articles of furniture to be found in the parlor will be far different from those found in the kitchen. This is only normal. Some articles will be made of precious metal while others will be made of much cheaper material.

So it is also in the church. There are those who have advanced far in sanctification. Those are of silver. Again there are others who are struggling. These are of cheaper material. But, there are also some unto dishonor. There are also hypocrites in the church, those who do not belong there.

Some things in a house, too are ready to be discarded. Jesus spoke of both wheat and tares in His kingdom. This is the kind of church in which the ministry of Timothy will take place.

Conduct required

How must Timothy now conduct himself in the ministry to such a church? He must not fall into the errors of those who bring dishonor to the church. He must purge himself from these and from their sins. There is always the danger that these people will influence others for evil.

Timothy must keep himself pure. Paul is not afraid of such statements. Many would say today that no one can purge himself — that is God's work. Of course, the Apostle does not teach here that a man is able to work his own salvation or that he is able to add anything to it. He simply emphasizes Timothy's own responsibility. If he keeps himself clean from the influence of evil men, he will be a vessel of honor, meet for the Master's use, and prepared to every good work.

Although Paul uses many illustrations in his writings, he never allows the illustration to bind him in any way. So here too; he goes far beyond the illustration he has used. No vessel in a household is able to change from one material to another but that is possible in the house of God. The reality rises far above the figure employed. No illustration can adequately picture the riches of the ways of God!

To be able to do the work of a pastor properly the minister must not only consider the work which has been assigned him but must also look closely at his own life. Paul warns his spiritual son concerning youthful lusts. We would almost conclude that Timothy was not susceptible to such things. He is pictured as timid, not forward, and possessed of a deep spirituality. Yet, the Apostle warns him.

The lusts referred to include the whole series of sins which may characterize youth. There are temptations which are stronger in youthful lusts are so dangerous because of immaturity. Mature years will often serve to blunt the force of temptation. Timothy must know his weaknesses. and run away from the youthful lusts. Fleeing these lusts he must pursue righteousness, faith, love and peace. These positive virtues which he must seek give us an indication of the nature of the youthful lusts by revealing their opposites. Timothy must live with the people of God on a high moral plane so that his own life will never be a barrier to the reception of the gospel.

Wrong teachers

Once more the Apostle refers to the foolish and ignorant questionings of some so-called teachers, of which he has spoken again and again. Those who engage in that type of teaching are splitting hairs. The Pharisees had done this for years. Jesus had warned the people of His day against such teachers because they made the burdens of life heavy for the people and they themselves did not even try to keep the numerous precepts they taught.

That kind of teaching is foolish. It also betrays ignorance of the important things. These teachings only bring strife and dissension. They are not based on objective truth and everyone of these teachers is his own authority — hence, strife. Timothy must refuse such things; he must not bother himself about them because there is no standard for refutation, i.e., there is no common ground on which you can meet.

Gentleness vs. strife

The fact that such teachings gender strife is sufficient reason to refuse them because the servants of the Lord must not strive, says Paul. This is a rather unexpected statement coming from a man who had been in the thick of strife his whole life. Never did he back away from the battles for the gospel. He was not only the defender of the faith but he also attacked unbelief in every form. This "soldier" of Jesus Christ now tells Timothy that the Lord's servant must not strive. Isn't this the very opposite of the way in which he has always conducted himself? Or is he simply accommodating himself to the fact that Timothy is useless for such a warfare?

It is true that Paul was always ready to do battle for the sake of the gospel against anyone who would oppose it. However, this was also the man who ministered to the church of Corinth in all meekness! If necessary — be ready to fight to the death! If it is not absolutely necessary — His servants must not strive but be gentle, etc. The teaching and influence of the heretics to which Paul had referred are not worthy of the striving of Christ's servants. Each must weigh the evidence carefully to determine when strife is necessary and when it is forbidden.

The man of God must be gentle, i.e., tolerant. The people must be able to approach him. They must be able to come to him with their problems. In this way he will be able to teach. There will be good rapport. He must be patient. His teaching will not always have the desired effect at once. This must not discourage him. He must be meek and that meekness will often be put to the test. Yet, this is the only way those who are teaching those foolish and ignorant things can ever be corrected. Striving with them will do no good. Instead, correct them with the positive teachings of the gospel. Our own attitude must not stand in the way.

The goal

This is not only the most sensible way of dealing with such people, but the goal too may not be lost from sight. That goal is their repentance, or rather, conversion.

One must not write off such people as difficult individuals

The Work of a Pastor

to deal with for whom there is no hope. The grace of God is able to do all things. His servants must, therefore, use the approved means in dealing with such people so that no stumbling block will be placed before them. If God is pleased to convert them there will be a complete turnabout. Paul himself is a good example of what the grace of God is able to accomplish. Through conversion they will turn from the foolish and ignorant to the knowledge of the truth. His servants are simply the instruments God employs to effect this transformation.

Through the proper instruction and the hoped for conversion, such people will return to soberness — they will come to their senses. Sin is irrational and the unconverted is "beside himself." Only the truth sets free completely. Only by coming to the true faith — only by true conversion will men free themselves from the snares of the devil. The devil lured them there while they thought they were their own masters. No, the devil has them captive and imposes his will on them. There is no power on earth or under the control of man which is able to deliver them. Besides, they don't realize themselves that deliverance is necessary. It is only the power of God which is able to set them free. This He accomplishes through conversion!

Although no man can ever boast that he has converted someone, God is pleased to use His servants, as instruments in His hand, equipped with the Word of God to accomplish this miracle. What a task! What a responsibility! Don't let any personality weakness of yours or sins of your youth stand in the way of the work of God, Timothy! Deny self and be filled with all the virtues of the true man of God so that His church may be built! The work of a pastor has been given an important place by God Himself in the accomplishment of His purposes.

Questions for discussion:
1. Illustrations are useful tools for a speaker or writer to make a matter plain. Can they also be dangerous? Explain.
2. Can an overemphasis on election make men careless? How can we maintain the proper balance?
3. Is it difficult to know when we ought to do battle and when we should be meek? A Luther and Calvin were faced with this problem; are we ever placed in that position?
4. What is the difference between regeneration and conversion? Is it important to maintain this distinction?

Lesson 6

The Coming Times

II Timothy 3:1-9

Man has an insatiable curiosity concerning the future. What will life and the world be like tomorrow, ten years from now? Usually an optimistic view is presented because, if we have come so far in the past, the future should be even better.

The Bible does not present such an optimistic view concerning the life of the people of God in their relation to their fellowmen. Grievous, i.e., difficult times are to be expected.

"The last days"

The term "last days" is used in different senses in the New Testament. Sometimes it means the days just before the Second Coming of our Lord. It is also used time and again to mean simply the "future." Joel also speaks of Pentecost as the last days. Paul considers himself to be living in the "end of the ages." Only the context of a passage can give us the meaning of the term whenever it is used.

Here the writer warns Timothy about these "last days." In other words, Timothy will experience them and should be on his guard. Here the term is, therefore, not restricted to the end of time.

Lawlessness

The characterization which Paul gives of the thinking and attitude of people in the "last days" is the direct opposite of the teaching of the law of God. Therefore he has placed so much emphasis on correct teaching or doctrine because the right teaching will lead to the proper life and false teaching leads to lawlessness.

The law of God demands that men shall love God above all and the neighbor as self. The people of the "last days" will be lovers of self, of money, and of pleasure. Hereby is their whole philosophy of life clearly shown. All the other things said about them follow logically. Once a person has turned his back to God's law, lawlessness, or the law of the jungle is followed. The men become boastful and haughty and railers. They become disobedient to parents — a totally unnatural attitude. They are thankful for nothing because they consider all things to be theirs as a matter of right. Their attitude is unholy — it is blasphemous.

"Without natural affection"

The people of that day will be without natural affection. Indeed there is a natural affection in this world. The relation of parent to child or the relation of husband and wife. However, those who are disobedient to their parents show that they have lost all natural affection. What is left to the individual when he has so broken with the law of God? He becomes implacable, i.e., irreconcilable, he begins to slander others, he is undisciplined, no self-control, he becomes fierce — untamed, like a wild animal. Of course they do not love the good nor do they love God, the highest Good! They become traitors, headstrong, and they believe that they are in the right. They live for themselves and have lost sight of the purpose of life.

The Apostle does not say that these things mentioned above *might* occur in the "last days," but that they *will* occur. The law of God has been given to prevent man's destruction of himself. The measure in which men disobey the law of God is the measure in which they lose their humanity! It is the moral law for the moral creature. Man cannot live without it. The "antichrist" or the "man of sin" is also called "the lawless one." Complete disobedience to the law of God is diabolical, devilish. It is therefore of such great importance that Timothy, and all who follow him, proclaim true doctrine and hold the law before the people constantly! Anyone who claims that the law was only for a former time and is not relevant for us today has never understood the Scriptures and is walking a very dangerous path.

"A form of godliness"

We would almost assume that the fearful conditions which the Apostle has described in the first four verses of this chapter refer only to the unbelieving world of the "last days." However, he tells us that *these same people* hold to a form of godliness! How can that be? How can people who deny the law, who make a mockery of the teaching of Scripture, still hold to a form of godliness? Yet, that will be the situation. This will make it far more difficult for Timothy and others to deal with the problem.

Such lawless people will be in the church! These are the ones who will tell Timothy that he must be more *tolerant* to the new times and circumstances. When one looks again at the long list of evils wherewith the Apostle charges them, it becomes very evident that they are most *intolerant!* Why do they seek to maintain a "form of godliness?" Superficially: for appearance's sake; basically: to undermine the church. They cling to some form of religion, but, of course, they have denied the power of it. It has no meaning for them. It doesn't change their lives; it doesn't lead to repentance.

Timothy must turn away from such people. He must not be blinded by their form of godliness, but must judge them by their fruits. It will be difficult to deal with these people because they are hypocrites, i.e., actors. They will deceive many. Especially the first key of the Kingdom of heaven, the preaching of the Word, must unmask them.

"Silly women"

Not only must Timothy turn away from such as make themselves guilty of the sins the Apostle has enumerated, he must also be aware of the fact that they will seek to lead others astray.

The example Paul uses may not be too clear immediately. However, it was clear to Timothy. As Paul describes it, these people will come to a home when the husband is absent. The women to whom he refers are "silly" or weak-minded. They do not have a good grasp of the truth' nor do they understand the implications of the truth for their lives. They are women who have come out of heathenism and their earlier lives were "laden with sin." The "new" teaching has a certain appeal to them because it seeks to free the conscience from guilt feelings.

So these women are always learning new things, but do not have a grasp of the truth. A grave danger exists that they will succumb to the evil teachings of these people and lead their families away from the truth. Therefore must Timothy proclaim the truth of God to unmask these false teachers and to guard the members of the church lest they too fall into the same error.

Jannes and Jambres

The Apostle now refers to the history of the Old Testament people of God to make it even clearer what the nature and purpose of these false teachings really are. He mentions Jannes and Jambres who withstood Moses. When we go to the Old Testament, however, we will not find these names. The names are found in the extra-Biblical literature of the Jews and in early Christian literature. Both Paul and Timothy are acquainted with this literature. According to this literature, Jannes and Jambres belonged to the wise men who were counselors to the Pharaoh of Egypt before whom Moses did his signs. Even when Moses commanded the plagues to come on the land, they did the same thing. Not till the third plague did they confess their inability to do the same wonders as Moses. They therefore withstood Moses. They attempted to negate the message of Moses. They did marvelous things and, no doubt, there were those who could see no difference between Moses on the one side, and Jannes and Jambres on the other side.

So do these lawless ones also withstand the truth. Their form of godliness must not deceive the people. In their opposition to the true doctrine they are withstanding the truth of God Himself. They are corrupted in mind because, apparently, they believe their own teaching to be true. The mind, which is able to receive and understand the Word of God, has been so corrupted within them that they cannot distinguish the lie from the truth. Of course, such people are reprobate concerning the faith. If they are so corrupted in mind that truth and falsehood are indistinguishable, Timothy must be able to distinguish between true and false members of the church. All that is called "church" or "faith" must be tested by Divine revelation.

Ultimate optimism

Although the Bible is not optimistic concerning the life of believers in the "last days," it does teach the ultimate optimism. That optimism is grounded in the fact that God rules and He will never allow anyone to take that rule out of His hand; and that Christ Himself has promised that His church shall be safeguarded to the end.

Paul therefore does not only tell his own son in the faith that the coming days will be evil. The evil of the coming days must not be minimized, but it is not the final note of history. They (the lawless ones) can only proceed as far as Christ allows them to go. It will become apparent to the people that their "folly" is diametrically opposed to the truth of God.

The history to which Paul had referred made this clear too. Moses showed miracles to Pharaoh — so did his opponents. These were to be Moses' credentials that God had sent him — his opponents undermined his Divine mission. However, the third plague (dust turned to lice) left his opponents helpless. God has seven more! The folly of those who wrest the word of the truth should become evident to all men. Yet, many have often fallen victim before this evidence dawns on them. Therefore hold fast the truth and proclaim it! Hold the law of God before all men lest they destroy themselves!

Questions for discussion:
1. Man was made to be able to remember the past but not to look into the future. Would you rather this reversed?
2. Does the Bible give us sufficient knowledge concerning the future? Does its revelation of the future bring fear of comfort?
3. Are the sins mentioned in the first five verses of this chapter quite common in our days? How should the church react?
4. Why do the evils spoken of in this section have an appeal? Can you imagine such people still being members of a church?
5. Why do many ungodly people still desire to have a minister lead the funeral service at the time of the death of a family member?
6. Do you think it is important to have knowledge of the extra-Biblical literature of former days?

Lesson 7

Encouragement in Difficulties

II Timothy 3:10-13

If the future days are to be characterized in the way Paul has done in the first nine verses of this chapter, what will become of Timothy? He will have to give leadership in the church of Christ during such days. Will he be able to stand in such times?

Timothy might even have a difficult time when there isn't a cloud in the sky and how will he fare when he will have to "contend with horses?" (Jer. 12:5) Paul is seeking to encourage him when difficulties come and to arm him for the warfare of those days.

Paul's teaching

Paul first of all shows the contrast between the enemies of the cross as they reveal themselves in the "last days" and the life of Timothy till the present time. He has been a follower of the Apostle and has patterned his own life after his. It was, therefore, the relation of teacher and disciple as well as missionary and successor. He was certainly aware of all the things which happened to Paul but also accepted that life as a model for himself. Paul often urges the churches to follow his example. This desire has been fulfilled in Timothy, as might be expected.

First of all, Timothy has followed Paul's teaching. This was the gospel of Jesus Christ of which he had been made a minister. This was the same teaching which had been entrusted to Timothy. He had not merely followed that Apostolic teaching as an interested spectator, but had *adopted* that teaching.

Paul's conduct and purpose

Likewise, Timothy had followed the conduct of his teacher. He saw that that conduct was in complete harmony with the things he taught. This is the opposite of hypocrites who teach one thing and conduct themselves in a different manner. So had Timothy also learned to live. The manner of life was determined by the gospel. That gospel had so gripped both of them that the whole life was permeated by it.

Paul's purpose had always been clear. He had a goal in life. That goal was so clear and so, important that every part of life and every moment had to bring him closer to it. He had given expression to that goal when he asked his Lord, Who appeared to him as he was about to enter Damascus: What wilt Thou Lord have me to do? In all of the remainder of his life he sought to do that will. "It is no more I that live; Christ Jesus lives in me." He has surrendered himself so completely to his Savior that he sees no other purpose than to glorify Him.

Now, you, Timothy, have followed my purpose and it is yours too. His faith has been evident to all. Timothy has seen that faith revealed again and again. He reads it in the letters he has received. That faith is grounded in his teaching, in the gospel. He lives out of that faith and therefore his conduct and purpose of life are what they are. The fruits of that faith are evident.

Timothy has been given that faith too. Timothy has seen how patient his teacher was with people. Therein too he was a true follower of his Lord. The love he had shown to the churches and to his intimate friends cannot be denied. The difficulties he had endured were all known to Timothy. These gifts had also been given to Timothy so that inwardly he is equipped to deal with difficulties as they arise. Therefore, stir up the gift of God which is in thee! You are not defenseless.

Encouragement in Difficulties

Paul's persecution

However, the Apostle has not yet concluded the catalogue of things wherein Timothy has followed him and will have to follow him in the future. He is, of course, aware of all the persecutions Paul has endured in the past. His had not been the life of ease as his early training might have promised. In II Corinthians 11 he recounts some of the things which happened to him for the sake of the gospel. It is a list of brutalities and tortures.

So far Timothy has not suffered as much, but, it may come! He is also aware of the things which happened to Paul on his first missionary journey. He was opposed by the Jews at Antioch. He had to flee Iconium because they were about to stone him. At Lystra (Timothy's home town) they had stoned Paul and Barnabas so that the people thought they were dead. Timothy was well acquainted with all these experiences and was, therefore, also fully aware of the dangers in following Paul.

The writer mentions all of the foregoing to give encouragement to his son and successor for the days to come. It may be that Timothy will have to endure the things which were mentioned or worse. He has received the necessary spiritual gifts to be able to stand. Concerning the persecutions Paul says that the Lord delivered him out of all of them. This is difficult to understand. As he is writing these words he is in prison awaiting certain execution! But, the Lord delivered me out of them all! Surely, not out of this last one! — Or did he? Paul does not mean deliverance in the sense of preventing them. Nor in the sense of making them less severe. By deliverance he means that these persecutions did not separate him from his Lord! Then he has been delivered out of them all. He has promised that nothing shall be able to separate us from the love of God which is in Christ Jesus our Lord (Rom. 8:35-39). He Who promised it is faithful.

What an attitude to the difficult life he had experienced which is now ending in Nero's dungeon! Only true faith had made it possible for him to endure all these sufferings. The Lord had said to Ananias in Damascus that He would "show him how many things he must suffer for my name's sake" (Acts 9:16). It had now indeed been shown him!

Paul's experience is not an isolated case but is and will be the common lot of God's people. No, others may not experience it in the severity experienced by this Apostle, but they will have to realize that their cause is not a popular one and will be opposed by the world. Paul speaks of those who would live godly, i.e., the devout, the pious. These are the ones whose faith is living and active. They refuse to compromise their beliefs. They will not follow unbelievers in their way of life. This will bring about resentment on the part of the world. Unbelievers, or false believers, will feel that they and their manner of life are being judged by the devout. This will finally lead to persecution. When the light of the gospel shines through the life of true believers and unmasks the works of darkness, they, who love the darkness more than the light, rebel. Then they turn against those who have shown them the true way of life. His people must expect these nights and should not fret when persecution comes. No, the reward which is to be given His people is so great that Paul can even rejoice in tribulation. The goal makes the struggle worthwhile!

Paul's view of evil men

The believers of the "last days" should also see their favored position in contrast with those who have persecuted them. He refers to those who were mentioned before — especially in the first nine verses of this chapter. These he now calls evil men and impostors. They are in the employ of the evil one, and he is a hard taskmaster. They are also deceivers — they are not to be trusted. These people do not

Encouragement in Difficulties

improve as time goes on but they shall wax worse and worse. They will go from bad to worse. They have already done much evil. How much worse can they get? Really, there is hardly a limit. The believer shudders at the greatness of his own sin. How deep can those fall who have not been regenerated by the power of God! When the end of time comes, such evil shall become evident as many had not thought possible!

These opponents of the people of God shall go on deceiving. They will, no doubt, deceive various people. However, not only will they deceive others, they will also deceive themselves. Sin so blinds the heart and understanding that they believe their own lies. Sin also brings its own punishment. The Apostle is not speaking of a possible conversion of such "evil men." They are hardened in sin and humanly speaking conversion becomes impossible.

Difficult times are coming, indeed. But, such spiritual strength has been given that you will be able to bear the affliction. And, the Lord rescues you out of it. There is no comparison between the glorious life of His people, though persecuted, and the empty and condemned lives of those who persecute them. Who is as rich as that man in Nero's dungeon whose earthly life is about to come to an end? He will soon be with his Lord — which is far better!

Questions for discussion:
1. Can we also be too much concerned about the evil days to come? Will those also still be "days of grace?" Explain.
2. Paul is not afraid to hold himself up as an example to others. Is this dangerous? Can it be evidence of spiritual pride?
3. What do you think of Paul's view of "deliverance?"

II Timothy & Titus

Is this the secret of those who suffer much and yet are always happy?
4. Does evil grow? Explain.

Lesson 8

The Scriptures

II Timothy 3:14-17

If a believer is to remain standing in time of peril and persecution he must indeed possess inner strength. There must be that strength of heart and soul which is found only in those who have true faith. We do not have that strength by nature.

Learned from excellent teachers

Timothy is urged to abide in the things which he has learned and of which he has been assured. Those times will not demand anything different from that which he already has. He has been taught the *truth* and that is all he will need regardless of times or circumstances. It is not simply a truth which he has accepted with the mind, but, after learning it, he has also been assured of its power.

Timothy can be assured of the truthfulness and power of the things he has learned if he bears in mind who his teachers were. These were people with the best credentials. They themselves believed the things they taught and lived by those things and were ready to die for them. Paul had been his teacher! His mother and grandmother had been his teachers! To be instructed in the truth by one of the Apostles of the Lamb was surely a great benefit and honor. He spoke the Word of God. His mother and grandmother loved him dearly and would give him nothing but the best. He had no reason to doubt the sincerity of any of his teachers nor their motives. Now, then, abide in these things. Hold on to them!

From the time of infancy Timothy has bean instructed in

the sacred writings. The Jews were faithful in instructing their children. Although many people of that day were illiterate, this was not true among the Jews. They had schools very early in their history. Their most important early possession was the subject matter for teaching. They had the Word of, God as it was contained in the Old Testament.

It was *the* subject matter. Other people did not have this treasure. It gave the Jews a knowledge of their history, it showed them the promises of God for the future, it gave them a view of life, it gave them moral, ceremonial and civil laws, and it gave them the book of songs. What a wealth this people possessed! In all of this Timothy had been instructed since earliest days by his mother and grandmother.

Received by faith

Paul had also been instructed in these sacred writings from his infancy, but there was one major difference between Timothy's education. These sacred writings are not sufficient in themselves. They led Paul to persecute the church, thinking, on the basis of the Old Testament, that he was doing God service. These sacred writings will only make wise unto salvation if faith in Jesus Christ is present. Without that faith they will never satisfy.

That is clearly evident from Paul's life as well as in the life of unconverted Jews who cling to the Old Testament. But, Timothy has not only received the instruction in these sacred writings, he has also been given the necessary faith in Jesus Christ. That fear of God is the principle of wisdom! The shadows of the Old Testament have been illumined for him by the light as it is risen in Christ Jesus. Hold this fast! Abide in it!

Inspired of God

We now come to a most important verse in Scripture. It deals with the nature of the Bible and its inspiration.

The Scriptures

There has been some debate on the question whether it should be translated "all Scripture" or "every Scripture." I believe it makes little difference and both translations are possible.

It must be noted that "all or every Scripture" does not mean the same thing as "sacred writings" in the previous verse. By "sacred writings" were meant the Old Testament only while the "scripture" of verse 16 includes both the Old Testament and the writings of the New Testament which were completed at this time. These are all placed on the same plane by Paul. Timothy must realize that from a babe he had been taught the Word of God.

The letters of Paul with which Timothy is familiar as well as the letter now before his eyes, is also the Word of God! Therefore it will be sufficient for him regardless of the nature of the times and, coupled with faith, will — make him wise to salvation.

All the Scriptures are inspired of God, says the Apostle. They are God-breathed. They have their origin in God Himself. The doctrine of inspiration has given much difficulty throughout the ages and our own age is no exception. We are, after all, dealing with a "book" which was written by many different individuals over a long span of time. Some are so afraid that we will not do justice to the "human factor." It is, of course, true that the styles of the different authors differ greatly. The church has, therefore, insisted that we are not dealing with a mechanical inspiration, but, rather, an organic inspiration. God took the human authors as they were — in their own times and with their ability or lack of ability — and gave us *His Word*. He did not only inspire the *thought*, but *every word*! Paul bases a whole argument on the fact that a certain singular is used rather than a plural (Gal. 3). Christ says concerning the law that not a letter or part of a letter shall fail! (Matt. 5:18).

Trustworthy

Seeing that the Scriptures are the product of God Himself they are trustworthy. Were this not true, how could man "live and die happily?" The believer must have an unshakable foundation upon which to stand or his hopes will be dashed.

Those who cast doubt on the veracity of any part of the Scripture are undermining the faith of His people. If the truth of Scripture is called into question everything else falls with it. The believer will have nowhere to turn. Paul had suffered bitter persecution and is ready to die for the truth revealed to him in the Scriptures! Timothy, and all believers must hold fast to it for the days to come.

Profitable

To the Apostle there is no possibility that any part of the Scriptures should not be the Word of God. Because God is the Author, it is perfect! If God wrote it, it is infallible. Then only is it profitable and useful for the work of the church. It is to be Timothy's textbook! He must find all of his own strength for his own spiritual life in it — and he must feed the people entrusted to him with it. No substitute may be condoned. The Spirit uses the Word to instill faith in Jesus Christ and so makes them wise to salvation. Nothing else can do this. Men have found and used substitutes for the Word of God again and again, but the Spirit has never found a substitute!

To be preached and taught

Timothy must preach that Word and he must also teach it. The people are to be instructed in that Word so that they will *know* it. Only if the Bible is acknowledged as the inspired Word of God will it be profitable for teaching. Besides, this Bible will also be extremely profitable in all pastoral work which Timothy performs.

The Scriptures

By means of the Word Timothy will reprove those who are erring. It is not Timothy who says they are wrong, but God says so! It will also have to be used positively to correct that which has not attained that ideal in Jesus Christ. It will be profitable to train the people to whom he ministers in true discipleship. In all that he is called to do, Timothy will have to use the Word. Philosophy will not comfort and psychology will not touch the heart but the Word of God does both.

Leads to every good work

What will be the result of such ministerial and pastoral work? One who has a calling as Timothy should have a goal in mind. All of the spiritual labor bestowed on the church of Christ is aimed at equipping the people of God to their task.

Paul speaks of "the man of God" by whom he means all true believers. Under the new dispensation all God's people have become prophets and priests and kings. The wish of Moses is being fulfilled (Num. 11:29). They have a great task to perform in their own hearts, in their family circles, and in the world. To do this properly they must be nourished by the Word of their God. He is building His church. He does so from within and from without. The inspired Word of God must be ministered to them faithfully to equip them to their task. That Word is to mold their lives. That Word is to give them vision.

Those who are not fed with the Scriptures will never be able to do the work given them to do. If they are fed with the true food, they will be equipped to very good work. The divine Judge will pronounce their works to be good because they stem from a true faith, are done according to the law of God and to His glory, and are not based on their own opinions or on the precepts of men (Heid. Cat., Q. 91).

II Timothy & Titus

Questions for discussion:
1. Are our godly teachers properly honored? How can we improve this situation?
2. How soon should we begin to instruct our children? Should we emphasize memorization of Bible texts and songs? Is this done enough?
3. How would you define inspiration?
4. Is the Bible without errors? Explain.
5. Is it so serious if we do not believe some of the things stated in the first chapters of Genesis to be historically true? What would be your answer to those who say that these things have nothing to do with our salvation?
6. Can spiritual life grow by any other means than the Word of God?

Lesson 9

Preach the Word

II Timothy 4:1-8

In the previous chapter Paul had warned Timothy concerning the nature of the times to come and how he should guard himself against falling victim to the evils which are to come. This is possible because God has given His Word which is able to give him everything he needs.

In this last chapter of this brief letter Paul shows Timothy what else is required of him. First this Word must have gripped his own heart and will then enable him to stand in the evil day. But, Timothy is also called to a very special office. He must *preach* the Word which His God has spoken and which he believes without a doubt. In other words: he will not be able to stand in that evil day if he does not hold fast to that Word in his own life, and he must attack the coming evil with the preaching of that Word!

Preaching — God's method

Timothy must preach, herald, proclaim that Word. That Word must be expounded. It is not enough to give that Word to another in some form or other, but it is to be preached! Where the Word is preached, the Spirit has promised to be active. Things happen where the Word is preached. No substitute is permitted. Paul is familiar with the philosophy and poetry of his day; and, no doubt, Timothy is too. But, preach only the Word!

It might seem as though it is an oversimplification to imply that the preaching of the Word will be sufficient as a weapon against the evils which have been listed. Paul doesn't think so. This is the only advice he has for

Timothy, but it is also far more than advice. He charges him in the sight of God and Christ Jesus that he preach the Word. He places him under oath. Men may think lightly of the effectiveness of the preaching of the Word (and many still think so today) it is the method and manner which God has chosen.

Let not Timothy dare to use a different method. He will have to answer to his God and to the Christ Who is Judge. His appearing and His kingdom are coming. That appearing and Kingdom is also Timothy's hope. Looking forward to that, he must be faithful in preaching the Word which speaks of these things.

How to preach

The "how" of that preaching is also emphasized. Timothy should be ready to preach that Word at all times and should seek out the opportunities for preaching it. Let no opportunity be missed. He should apply it to the individual. He must reprove with the Word of God. He should rebuke sin and not allow it a place in the heart of the hearer.

The admonitions should be fatherly — not toned down, but given in a spirit of love. The Word must be taught and that teaching has to be accompanied by patience. They will not immediately grasp or apply the truth. The teacher and preacher must be long-suffering. He must be willing to teach and teach; to sow and sow, and perhaps have someone else reap.

"Itching ears"

Although the Apostle has also given a characterization of the coming times in the previous chapter, he now goes into greater detail to underscore the importance of the preaching of the Word. Timothy must realize that he is still able to preach it now and that there are also those who gladly listen to it. Therefore he must now use every opportunity to impress the truth of God on the hearts and minds of those he is able to reach. Because the time is coming when they will — not endure the sound doctrine. That sound, or healthy, doctrine is the one in which men will find life.

People will not want that doctrine in the coming days. They will have "itching ears," Paul says. They will want to hear that which seems pleasant to them. They will want to be entertained. Their "itching ears" will demand "scratching" to satisfy them. As a result they will have *many* teachers. No one person is going to be able to satisfy their desires. No one person will be so "creative" as to be able to come up with all the new "gimmicks" desired. They will "heap" to themselves such teachers.

Paul had been able to satisfy the church in his day. Timothy could also do this for the church in his time. But, when "itching ears" are more prominent than believing and obedient hearts, they will have to have many teachers, and all of them will not be able to satisfy. These are teachers who agree with the lusts of those they teach. Their lusts determine their teachers — rather than the calling of God for the building up in the faith to that full manhood which is in Christ Jesus.

Turning to fables

Of course, these have turned away their ears from the truth. The truth is become their enemy. The Word of God is not honored. But, when one turns from the truth, where can he go? The Apostle replies that they will turn aside to fables!

Mind you! The truth despised — and trust placed on fables! Yet, that is precisely the road of the unbeliever. When entertainment takes the place of worship, when philosophy and poetry become competitors for the Word of God, men have turned aside to fables and have left the truth.

Sober in all things

Seeing this is going to be the course of events, Timothy must preach the Word whenever opportunity is presented. When these times, as described by the Apostle, come, Timothy must remain sober. He must remain calm. He is not to feel as though all his work is now in vain. To harvest fruit is not his first calling; but, to be faithful. Let him then remain sober when sobriety has left all others.

Timothy must do the work of an evangelist. This is simply another term which the Apostle uses for the preaching of the Word. He must do his work, his calling, to the full. Even though he should have to suffer for it at the hands of men, nothing may cause him to swerve from his calling. Shall the preaching of the Word stem the tide of evil and apostasy? Yes, that Word will ultimately triumph, and therefore it must be preached!

Paul's example

Once more Paul uses himself as an example to encourage his son in the faith and his successor in the ministry. Will Timothy not give up the struggle when he sees what that same struggle has done to Paul? Only if he misinterprets what is taking place with the Apostle. Therefore Paul will now give him the proper interpretation of his own life in order that Timothy may be spurred on to renewed zeal.

Timothy knows, of course, what the situation is with Paul. Paul is also fully aware of the things he can expect. Notice how he speaks of his coming death. He doesn't use the term "death." No, his life is being poured out as a thankoffering. That kind of sacrifice had no salvational value, but it was added to the sacrifices as a token of thanks. So is his life now being poured out — in gratitude to his God! The time of his "departure" has come. He is about to be loosed, released. He will depart from the chains which now bind him. He will be released from the "body of

Preach the Word

this death." But, he will also depart from those who are very dear to him! Throughout the New Testament both of these elements are emphasized. Departure will indeed be release, but he does not advocate the inhuman sentimentality as though there were no place for tears.

Looking back, he says that he has fought the good fight. It was the fight that had to be waged — therefore good. He had not wasted his life striving about things of no value, but, at the same time, he had not shirked his duty when the truth was not to be defended. He has finished the course. The course of life is coming to the end. That course of life had not been an easy one. Jesus had set him on the course, and he had kept his eye on Jesus, Who is also the finisher.

Of course, the Apostle is using metaphors from the area of athletics. However, don't pay so much attention to the metaphor that the thing illustrated is lost from sight! He has kept the faith. By this he means his subjective faith. All his experiences in life have confirmed the faith. There you see him now! — a man about to be executed for the faith calmly telling Timothy to preach the Word so that others share in that assurance!

A glorious future

But, the Apostle hasn't finished his word to Timothy. He says, because I have so fought and so run, and because I still have the true faith, therefore He will give me a crown when I will stand before Him! That is the crown of righteousness, that is, the crown which is rightly mine because He promised it! *He is holding God to His promise!* The Lord, the righteous judge — He will give it to me in that day — the day of resurrection. Don't feel sorry for me, Timothy, I am departing to receive the crown!

Not only can the Apostle of the Lamb say this, No, Paul quickly adds: "and not to me only, but also to all them that have loved his appearing." All those who have kept the faith; all those whose cry of faith is: Come Lord Jesus; yea, come quickly; they shall receive that crown. What a glorious future! Therefore, Preach the Word! Nothing else can bring to this glorious end.

Questions for discussion:
1. Does "Preach the Word" include the many forms of "communicating" which are being used in many churches today? If not — is it then such an innocent method?
2. A few years ago many said that the day of preaching was past. The dialog was supposed to take its place. What do you think would be the answer of Scripture to these ideas?
3. The modern church has used "gimmicks" for years to get people to church. This failed. Why then do many churches do this today? Or don't they?
4. What does it mean to "hold God to His promises?" Do we do this enough?
5. Some seem to believe that every Christian sees death as a joyous event. How do you react to that?

Lesson 10

Paul's Last Words

II Timothy 4:9-22

The Apostle is coming to the end of this second letter he has written to Timothy. This was the last letter he wrote which was included in the canon of Scripture. There are many personal references now but his love for the church and his own relation to Christ shine through clearly.

Desire to see Timothy

Paul urges Timothy to make the long trip to Rome soon. Here indeed is the evidence of the Apostle's loneliness and his strong desire to see Timothy once more. There isn't too much time left so that Timothy should not postpone this journey any longer.

Although Paul's personal desire is very evident, there is, no doubt, also further reason — even though he does not express it in so many words. Paul will have a lot of advice and counsel for Timothy. He has written two letters, but there are certain things which are best communicated mouth to mouth. Come soon, Timothy.

Deserted by Demas

Paul's loneliness and thereby his desire for Timothy's presence — has also been increased by the desertion of Demas. This man had been a helper to Paul. He had even followed him to Rome, but, in time, he was not strong enough to stand with the Apostle. Paul says: He left me in the lurch. Paul had counted on his help and presence but that trust was misplaced. Demas loved this present world and left to go to Thessalonica. Paul does not say that he had become a gross sinner. Demas saw all that this present world can offer and contrasted that with the confinement of Paul — and — he made the wrong choice!

Another helper, Crescens, has gone to Galatia, and Titus to Dalmatia. These left for legitimate reasons. The work in the church of Jesus Christ has to continue. They cannot all stay with an imprisoned Apostle! Only Luke "the beloved physician" is with him now. Luke is a great help to him. In him he even has a personal physician. But, Luke is especially a companion to him — an educated and cultured man who shares Paul's deepest beliefs.

Asks for John Mark

Timothy is also asked to bring John Mark with him to Rome. The mention of this name brings back memories. At one time Mark had deserted Paul on his missionary journey. Seeing Mark was not dependable, Paul refused to take him on the second missionary journey. This even gave rise to some bitterness between Paul and Barnabas. As a result, Paul took Silas and Barnabas took Mark. Later Mark proved himself and the Apostle no longer holds the former experience against him but tells Timothy that Mark is useful to him in the work he is still able to do.

Sends Tychicus to Ephesus

To do that which Paul desires, i.e., for Timothy to go to Rome to visit him, will bring many difficulties. It is a long and slow journey. It is not a matter of days or weeks, but of months! It may indeed be very profitable for Timothy to be able to speak with Paul face to face, but how can a minister be away from his work so long? Timothy will not leave the church that long and give his people a prey to all the evils which have been mentioned before. Paul realizes this.

Paul tells Timothy that he doesn't have to worry about the church in his absence because he has already sent Tychicus

Paul's Last Words

to Ephesus to take his place. This is a trusted servant of God and the Ephesian church will be well cared for in Timothy's absence.

Needs cloak, books, parchments

In a letter such as this one there are naturally some things of a very personal nature which have little meaning for a later time. Thus Paul speaks later of greeting various individuals who are totally unknown to us.

Seeing that Paul expects Timothy to come, he asks him to bring the cloak which he had left at Troas with a certain Carpus. Winter is approaching and the heavy cloak will be very welcome. Besides, he should bring the books and parchments. It is useless to speculate which books and parchments these were. Timothy knew which ones he meant and we do not. These words are important only in that they reveal to us the Apostle's concern for both his physical and mental well-being.

Beware of Alexander

Paul also refers to a certain Alexander who had done him much harm and had greatly withstood his words. This man is also unknown to us. Paul does not give us a detailed description of evil things this man had done. But, he had done "much evil" — he had brought great damage to Paul's defense. He had "greatly withstood" the words of Paul. This man was a metalworker — not a scholar, but nevertheless a man on whom he had depended.

Paul has no vengeful spirit but simply says that the Lord will render to him according to the things he did. Vengeance belongs to the Lord. However, he warns Timothy to beware of this person. The way in which this man has treated Paul is on his own conscience; he will not seek vengeance, but will turn the other cheek. But his past deeds should certainly teach Timothy not to trust him!

Forsaken by men

The following verses present somewhat of a problem regarding the time of which Paul is speaking. Is he speaking of the present imprisonment in which there may have been more than one defense? I believe, however, that he now refers to his first imprisonment from which he had been set free. He refers to that time as an example for the present imprisonment. At that time no one came to his defense. There was the provision in Roman law for friends, family, or acquaintances to plead the cause of the accused. This could, of course, be a great help for a prisoner. It also involved danger for those who would defend him because the "link" between them and the accused might make them suspect.

No one defended Paul at that time; no, they all forsook me! They were no heroes! Paul prays that these deeds — or this negligence — may not testify against them when they stand before their Judge. Here he assumes a different attitude than the one he took against Alexander. These, who could have spoken the proper word at the proper time, loved Paul and his cause. They were simply afraid. Alexander, on the other hand, was an enemy of the cross.

Not forgotten by the Lord

Although no one stood by Paul during that first defense, the Lord had not forgotten him. He always remains faithful. He is also the most important Helper. He stood by me and He strengthened me, says Paul.

That strengthening was necessary for Paul too. One would certainly lose all hope and courage if he had to rely on self or fellow-men. Because of the Lord's aid at that time the message of the gospel could again go forth through the instrumentality of Paul. He had used the time given him. He had not toned down the gospel to prevent further difficulty with the authorities, but had boldly declared the

Kingship of Jesus Christ by word of mouth and by epistle. He had indeed been rescued out of the mouth of the lion.

The present imprisonment is quite different from the first. Paul is fully aware of this fact, but, nevertheless, boldly states that the Lord will deliver him again. The former time he had been delivered to take up his Apostolic work again; now He will save me unto His heavenly kingdom. This too is deliverance. The Lord remains faithful. That is the God Who is to be praised forever!

Sends greetings

Timothy must give the greetings of Paul to various people who have labored with him in the gospel. First of all, Prisca (or Priscilla) and Aquila. These people had been a great help to Paul in the past and had instructed Apollos in the truth as it is in Christ. Greet Onesiphorus, a man who had befriended Paul and sought him out when he was in Rome. Erastus, whose name is also mentioned in Acts, is now in Corinth, so he cannot send greetings.

Trophimus was left behind in Miletus, sick. This is an interesting observation. Paul healed many sick and even raised some from the dead. However, he was not able to use that power at will nor was the faith of the sick person decisive. The miracles were performed for the purpose of revelation and redemption! Paul would not — have left this trusted helper at Miletus sick in the time when every help was needed in the church.

He pleads with Timothy to come before winter. The long sea journey will be far more dangerous during the winter; Paul's time is running out; and he needs the cloak. Do everything in your power to come before winter.

In closing he mentions four persons who send their greetings to Timothy. We do not know any one of them, but, of course, they were known to Timothy. It doesn't help us to know the meaning of the names because those names in the Greek and Latin world of that day had no more meaning than today. All the brethren at Rome salute Timothy.

Final benediction

Paul now lays a final benediction on his beloved son. The Lord be with thy spirit. Then you won't need anything else. This is a declaration — not a prayer. Grace be with the church. Paul is brief, but everything is included in these few words. He hopes to see him — but — God's will be done and His faithfulness will always uphold Timothy and the church.

Questions for discussion:
1. Do you think we would have known the personality of Paul as well if he had not written the verses 9-22 of this chapter?
2. How does Paul show a forgiving spirit regarding Mark? Does it detract from a forgiving spirit if we demand proof of change?
3. Do you think the teaching of Christ concerning the turning of the other cheek and going the second mile is often misinterpreted? Would you say that a misinterpretation of this teaching can make Christianity absurd?
4. What do you think of the efforts of some to find a "deeper meaning" in the cloak and books and parchments?
5. Paul is lonely, yet fearless in the face of death. Is this logical? Explain.

Titus

Lesson 11

Greetings and Purpose

Titus 1:1-9

One has to do some searching in the New Testament to find out who and what kind of person Titus was. His name is not even mentioned in the Book of Acts. Paul does mention his name several times in II Corinthians and in Galatians, makes one reference to him in II Timothy, and now writes an epistle to him. However, Titus played a very important role in the history of the early New Testament church.

Person and Role of Titus

According to Galatians Titus had been in close contact with Paul already during Paul's first missionary journey. The Apostle took him along to the Synod of Jerusalem (Acts 15). Here Titus was used as a test case. In the opinion of many of the leaders in the church at that time, circumcision was necessary before one would be accepted in the church. Paul had allowed Timothy to be circumcised so that he would not be a stumbling block to the Jews. However, if they are going to *demand* circumcision for entrance into the church of Christ, Paul will never agree! One of the important decisions of this Synod was to declare that faith alone is necessary to salvation.

Paul had used Titus to bring both of the Epistles to the Corinthians to that church. This meant not only to deliver the letters the Apostle had written, but it also involved giving advice and leadership to that church in the name of the Apostle. The leadership qualities of Titus and the confidence Paul has in him are thereby clearly shown. He does not have the fearful spirit of a Timothy, but he is

II Timothy & Titus

able to go ahead on his own. Both his parents were Greeks and he had, no doubt, been converted under the preaching of Paul.

This letter is written to Titus while he is laboring in Crete. Most likely it was written to him between Paul's first and second imprisonment. There are many similarities between the first letter to Timothy and this one, but there are also many new things. Because the time of the writing of this letter is late in the life of Paul, the church had already come to quite full organization. Titus is urged to work diligently for the development of his people in the faith.

Salutation

Although we are accustomed to the manner in which Paul begins his various epistles, the salutation on this one is much longer than usual. By this means he makes it very clear that, although it is addressed to an individual person, the letter is intended for the church and is normative.

Paul is the servant or slave of God. He belongs to his Maker. This is the same thought as expressed in the first question and answer of the Heidelberg Catechism. He is not his own, but belongs to Another. This is also his only comfort.

But, this is not only true of Paul as a believer but is especially true because of the office to which he has been called. He is Apostle of Jesus Christ! It never ceases to amaze him that he has been called to this task and he always holds this office in high esteem. His Apostleship is exercised in behalf of the faith of God's people. He ministers to the chosen ones of God. It is the office which he employs to establish God's people in the truth. This involves the proclamation of the Word. That truth brings forth godliness and it alone gives the hope of eternal life.

The truth of God has been "one" from the beginning. God gave His promises from the beginning of the revelation.

Greetings and Purpose

The promise was salvation. But, it took so long! There seemed to be so little progress for thousands of years. Yet, the God who made the promise cannot lie. Now it is revealed!

The "Mystery" has been clarified. He made known the fullness of salvation at the right time.

Paul was now entrusted with that word of the fulfillment of all promises. This had been given to him at the command of "God our Savior." In Paul's vocabulary both God and Christ may be called "Savior." Christ has come to bring salvation and may therefore be called the Savior of men. God the Father made it possible by sending His Son in the flesh and He too may be called our Savior.

After this rather long introduction Paul now finally addresses the one to whom the letter is written. He writes to Titus, who, like Timothy, is his child in the faith. Spiritually Paul has begotten Titus. His feeling for the person of Titus also reminds one of the tender feeling he had expressed for Timothy. Sometimes the Apostle uses the triple blessing: grace, peace, and mercy in his letters. Here it is only "Grace and peace." Both salutations are proper and include all the blessings needed by the individual or church.

Duties of Titus at Crete

At the conclusion of the salutation the author immediately introduces the purpose of his writing. He has left Titus at Crete. Apparently the Apostle had also labored on this island, perhaps between the first and second imprisonment. However, Paul was not able to stay there until the church was well established. His missionary calling does not permit him to stay in any one place for any great length of time. There is so much to do and so little time to do it. He goes from place to place sowing the seed of the gospel. That is his primary calling. After the seed has been sown there is still very important work to be done — but that can be done by others. At Crete the work was not finished and he has left Titus there to set things in order. Titus is to build on the work begun by Paul and bring the church to greater development.

The first thing to be done for the well-ordering of the church is to have elders appointed in the church. No church will fare well if it does not have men who have been ordained for the specific purpose of watching over the flock. This was Paul's custom in all the churches. Seemingly he had been at Crete such a short time that he had not had the time to appoint such elders. Titus must now see to it that this be accomplished.

Qualifications of elders

In the other Pastoral Epistles the Apostle has also spoken of the qualifications of officebearers, but he does so again in writing to Titus. Some of these qualifications, naturally, are the same as we find them elsewhere in his writings, and some new elements are emphasized here.

The church must be very careful in their choice of elders. Such a person must be of good report, he must be blameless in the eyes of men. A person concerning whom there are suspicions is not qualified. He is to be the husband of one wife. This was an important matter in that day of polygamy. One who had more than one wife at the time of his conversion might be tolerated as a member of the church, but he could not serve as an elder. His moral character must be beyond reproach.

Similarly, the elder should not have an ungodly family. If his children are still in heathendom and live accordingly, he is not qualified to be an elder. Once more the Apostle states that he must be blameless, and now particularly in regard to his own personality. The gospel of Jesus Christ must have changed his personality to conform to the demands of Christ. Self-will, temper, wine-lover, fighter,

Greetings and Purpose

greedy person — none of these characteristics may be found in one who is entrusted with the welfare of the church.

What kind of a person must an elder be? He has to be given to hospitality. This was an important matter at this time in the history of the church. It also agreed with the ancient Jewish custom. There were so many who travelled from one place to another, either for the promotion of the gospel, or because they were persecuted from one place to another. An elder's home should be open to such. He should love to do those things which are a blessing to others. He should have that wisdom which is born of the gospel. So only will he be able to solve the various problems whereby he may be faced in his office. He must be fair in judgment; he must live by faith himself; and he should always be in control of himself. Some of these qualifications are strictly spiritual and others are personal. Both must be present.

For his work the elder must be well instructed in the truth of the Word of God. We would now expect that he would say: "The teaching which is according to the faithful word," but, instead, he says: "Holding to the faithful word which is according to the teaching." The word to which he refers here is the preaching of the word. That word must be according to the teaching of the church. In other words, he must know the confession of the church which is based on the revelation of God, and must judge the preaching he hears in that light. Then he must also hold to the true preaching! So he will be instructed. The true preaching is to be his food and drink and he must be able to discern between the true and the counterfeit.

This proper relation to the Word will enable the elder to do his work. He will then be able to comfort the people of God with the truth. This is so necessary for the development of the faith of God's people. The elder must first receive before he can give. He will then also be able to defend the truth against those who are opposed to it.

II Timothy & Titus

Questions for discussion:

1. Was Paul inconsistent in agreeing to the circumcision of Timothy and opposing it in the case of Titus? Explain.
2. How important is it to know something of the author, the person addressed, the time and purpose of a book of the Bible? Can we understand the words without this knowledge?
3. Would you object to be called a "slave" of Jesus Christ? What does it mean for our practical life to confess the truth of the Heidelberg Catechism, Question 1?
4. Can a church prosper without elders? How about the churches which have only a board of deacons?
5. Is discipline exercised on the basis of the Word or the Confessions?

Lesson 12

The Conditions at Crete

Titus 1:10-16

Titus, as well as every minister, should be fully aware of the nature of his congregation, the dangers which threaten, and the nature of the surroundings of the church.

Paul gives him a very vivid description of these matters in this section. From this description it will become clear why the church at Crete must have such qualified elders as he has spoken of in the former verses.

False teachers

In the church at Crete there are many problems which remind one of the problems spoken of in the Epistles to Timothy. There are unruly men, i.e., men who will not bow before the Word preached. These are vain-talkers they babble. They are deceivers. They give the impression that they know something while they know nothing. They believe themselves far more capable than Titus. They sit in judgment on the truth. Especially the Jews in the church at Crete (and there were many Jews there) make themselves guilty on this score. These people have a long history of religion and now consider themselves capable of teaching all others.

Their mouths must be stopped, says the Apostle. They may not even be allowed to continue in their evil work. Even though Paul does not tell Titus in so many words how this is to be done, Titus will realize that the discipline of the church is to be used to silence these false teachers. Their teaching is not an innocent sport — they are overthrowing whole families. People are being led astray by their unscriptural teachings. This may not continue. They must be muzzled. These teachers are not even engaged in their teaching for principal reasons of their own, but they are doing it to enrich themselves!

Cretans an evil people

The author now shows Titus how serious this matter is and why it arises. He speaks in a very un-Paul-like way. He quotes one of the poets of Crete, Epimenedes; who had given an unflattering characterization of his own people. As is also evident from other Pauline writings, the Apostle was well-acquainted with the Greek and Roman literature. He calls Epimenedes one of their own prophets, i.e., one of their own teachers or poets. Such a person might be expected to overlook the faults of his own people and praise them for many different things. That is, however, not the case. This "prophet" of theirs had come with a withering criticism of his own people. Cretans, he said, are always. liars, evil beasts, idle gluttons! These are, of course, generalizations. Paul usually does not make sweeping generalizations. Yet, he tells Titus that what this man said about the Cretans is true. You cannot depend on them. The lie is a way of life for them. They have a reputation for being liars. They are also cruel — evil beasts. Those who have no respect for truths usually have no respect for the feeling of others. They are also gluttons — lazy, pleasure-mad and sensuous. What a characterization to give of a whole people! However, it is such a well known fact that this "prophet" has spoken the truth about his own people that the Apostle dares to agree with this appraisal.

Reproof needed

Titus must, therefore, realize that he will have to deal with difficult people. He must not think that the evils in the church will disappear all by themselves They must be

The Conditions at Crete

reproved sharply. At different times the Apostle has urged the application of discipline in the churches. However, the manner in which the discipline is to be exercised will differ according to the nature of the offense and the nature of the guilty person.

These people in Crete must be reproved sharply. Nothing less will do. They are to be led back to the true faith — not only in confession, but also in practice. Discipline should always seek the restored health of the individual. He must again become "sound" in the faith. At the same time the church may not be left in the danger of falling into the heresies of these deceiving teachers. Titus will indeed need qualified elders to deal with such problems!

Jewish fables

The situation on Crete would be bad enough if Titus had only to deal with the "Cretan mind," but it becomes even worse when the Jews come with their fables. These are the trifling matters — matters which have no importance, empty. They have also come with the many commandments of men as they were taught by the Pharisees.

The gospel has set men free from all these added commandments. Don't listen to them! They turn men away from the truth. The "more strict" interpretation of these Jewish teachers is not a sign of greater spirituality, but of blind error. Christ has set us free so we may rejoice in His service.

Danger of external religion

Now follows a statement which has the force of a proverb. Yet, we do not read it earlier in the Scriptures. Paul says; To the pure all things are pure. What does that mean? Does it mean that a person is his own standard of purity? Some think so. However, this Apostle has always stressed the fact that the Word and law of God alone are normative. I, even as a believer, may think something to be perfectly proper. But, the only thing that counts is: what does the Word or the Law say? Surely, Paul does not mean that even the pure person is a law unto himself! This kind of statement must be treated very carefully lest we fall into grave error. It is the kind of statement which is often quoted out of context and made to say the opposite of that which the Bible teaches.

To come to a proper understanding of this statement it must be seen in the context in which it is used. Paul has been writing about the errors which the Jews brought into the church. These people had been brought up to differentiate between the clean and the unclean — between the pure and the impure. These things were deeply impressed on them and formed a large part of their religious life. There was always the lurking danger that their whole religion would become externalized. If they were obedient in the things commanded in the ceremonial law, everything was in order. The prophets came to them time and again to warn them that external observance was not enough. The heart had to be in tune with their God!

In the days when Jesus was on earth, the Pharisees had become masters at emphasizing the externals. Christ condemned this teaching. Now, in the early church, this same leaven was still operating. Therefore Paul says: To the pure all things are pure. Only the pure of heart are the ones who are truly obedient. He makes this clear in the following statement. To the defiled and unbelieving, nothing is pure. To such people the clean animal is not pure! Now that the ceremonial law has been done away, even the formerly unclean animal is clean to the pure in heart! So Paul can use this statement as a proverb. Seeing that nothing is pure to such as seek their religious comfort in the ceremonial law, and then only in its external observance, both their minds and consciences are defiled. Their minds do not grasp the

The Conditions at Crete

truth of the gospel and their judgments are wrong.

The Jews with their long history of the true religion, the people of the promise, the people who had received the law of God and to whom the oracles of God were given, believed that they knew God. They profess to know Him. The nations around them worshiped idols — and these were no gods. Surely, the Jews may then profess that they alone know the true God. But, do they? When the Son of God came they did not recognize Him. Although God had indeed spoken to them as to no other people, they, by their own views of religion, had made a god in their own image. By their works they deny the true God. That God had not only spoken to them in the various ceremonies, but He had also made clear to them the need of redemption. This fact they had denied. They had only kept the ceremonies and thereby had killed all spiritually.

Despite their form of godliness the sad fact is that they are abominable in the sight of God. They have denied the power of true godliness. God requires more than mere external form. Despite the fact that they boast about their keeping of the law, they have become disobedient. They may still honor the letter of the law, but the spirit of the law is missing in them. What an indictment of those who pride themselves on their religious heritage and observance! Their religion, grounded in the revealed truth, has become false by their attitude toward it! The people who had received the promises, now oppose the church built on the fulfillment of promise. They are unfit for any good work. They are worthless — they cannot be used.

Paul usually went to the synagogue first when he came into a new city. He still has a deep love for his "kinsmen" Yet, how difficult they made his work. How injurious they were to the church of Christ. Titus, and the whole church, must realize that for the Jew too, the only way of salvation is through the blood of Jesus Christ!

Questions for discussion:
1. What are the purposes of discipline? What is their order of importance?
2. Should a minister be familiar with other than theological literature? Why?
3. May we ever make such generalizations as are found in verse 12?
4. What is Christian liberty? If a person says: I see nothing wrong in this, does that mean that it is not wrong for him?
5. By what process can true religion in the course of time become false? Are we in danger of this?
6. Is there a special place for the Jews still today? How is the Jew saved?

Lesson 13

The Christian Family

Titus 2:1-10

Titus had been instructed to remain in Crete so that those things for which Paul did not have time might be accomplished. First of all he had to see to it that elders were appointed in every church so that the church might be able to function properly. When elders, qualified elders, have been chosen, the emphasis can fall on the development of the spiritual life of the church.

An important unit in Society

In this section the Apostle stresses the need of building up the Christian family. The family is such an important unit in all society and also in the life of the church. The author does not lay down various general principles whereby the family is to be guided, but approaches the matter from the point of view of the responsibility of the various members of the family. This novel approach gives him the opportunity to say some things about the Christian family which might otherwise not come to light. It also reveals to the church of all time the duties of every family member.

Titus is urged to live a consistent life as the minister to the church on the island of Crete. In all his conversation he is to speak consistently with the preaching during worship. All his speaking and action must agree with the sound, healthy doctrine. Thus, he must not only make known to the people the way of salvation through the blood of Christ, but the implications of the gospel must be clearly taught. The sound doctrine must rule all of life — including the family relationships.

For mature men

First of all Paul speaks of the duty of the "aged men" in the family. It is difficult to say whether the concept — "aged men" — has the same meaning for Paul as it has for us. Nor is it so important to know which age level he had in mind. It is clear that he means mature men — those who have experienced a great deal in life.

Such men are to be temperate. They are not to be given to drink, nor are they to live in a manner which is not consistent with the faith they profess. They are to be grave and sober minded. They are to have a certain dignity as is consistent with their years. They are to be sound in the faith so that they may be able to teach those who are younger. They must also be sound in love, i.e., a love which shows kindness, and not the more intemperate love of those who are young. They have experienced much in their lives and it ought to be evident to all that the Christian mature man has learned to deal with the adversities of life as well as with the joys of life.

Youth is often impatient, but the progress of sanctification should make those who are older far more patient. So, these people, the aged men, will exert a very beneficial influence in the Christian family as they teach those who are younger by word and deed.

For mature women

Next the Apostle turns his attention to the place which the aged women occupy in the Christian family. Titus must urge them, in keeping with the teaching of the gospel, to be reverent. They are to "act their age" in both dress and deportment. That is the only way in which they will be able to do the things expected of them.

Of course, these women must not be slanderers — gossipers who ruin the reputation of others. In that time of intemperate drinking on the part of so many, Titus must

The Christian Family

also warn these older women not to be enslaved to wine. They must, by both word and deed, teach the truth and practical value of the teaching of the gospel.

For younger women

The influence of these mature Christian women is especially great in instructing the younger women. The teachers are those who no longer have the daily responsibility of a family. By their sanctified experience they can, and should be, a great help to the younger women who have many responsibilities every day in their family life.

How much such younger women can learn from those who have the experience and serve the Lord! They should be taught to love their husbands and children. The mother-love is the cement which binds the family together! Amid all the problems which arise over the years it may be difficult to maintain that love at the proper level, yet, if that love fails, the family is in jeopardy. These mothers must be sober-minded — they should show more and more maturity in dealing with the problems of life in a sensible manner. Of course, they must be chaste because unchastity destroys marriage, the home and family.

These Christian mothers should be workers at home. There is more than enough to do right in, their own home — in fact, there are not enough hours in the day for a mother of a family. To remain kind amid all the irritations which may arise is not easy — but necessary. They are to learn to be in subjection to their own husbands. Yes, even though there is considerable emphasis on the equality in marriage today, the Apostle tells Titus to urge the older women to teach the younger women to be subject to their husbands. That is necessary in a Christian family.

When Paul adds the words: "That the word of God be not blasphemed," he has reference to all that he has said in the previous verses - including the order to the younger women to be in subjection to their husbands. This teaching is not only found here but is in keeping with all of the teaching of the Scriptures. To go contrary to that word Paul calls blaspheming. If they go contrary to this word they will ruin the Christian family.

For younger men

The younger men in the family are urged to be sober-minded. They should place themselves in all their words and activities under the discipline of the Word of God. No Christian family is possible unless the members of that family live by the Word.

For Titus himself

There are also others, though not members of the immediate family, who will have considerable influence in strengthening the family tie. Titus himself must recognize his responsibility toward the families under his care. He must be an example to all of them. As a minister of the Word he must bring the whole counsel of God to the people. But, he has further responsibilities. He must be an example to them of good works. He must live the gospel!

Whether Titus is engaged in formal teaching or preaching, or if he is engaged in informal "talk" with his people, he is to see to it that he is a model for others to follow. He must always be the minister! Difficult? Of course — but necessary. By his teaching and preaching and living in such a way, the enemies of the cross will be put to shame and His people will take courage. Where precept and example are in full agreement, the unbelievers will have "no evil thing to say of us." Great harm can be done by the minister who does not live his confession.

For servants

Paul now refers to a group which, strictly speaking,

The Christian Family

doesn't belong to the family. Yet, he usually brings this group into the picture whenever he speaks of family relationships. He refers to servants or slaves. Although they are not members of the family, their attitudes and deportment will affect family relationship again and again. Some of these worked in the home and others worked in the fields. Again, he does not say anything about the institution of slavery directly, but his exhortations to the slaves — if obeyed — would have destroyed this institution in a short time.

Titus must instruct the servants to be obedient to their masters and by this obedience be well-pleasing to them. They are to render obedience in all things. Some wonder if they are also to be obedient when they have received orders to do wrong. Of course not. They must be obedient in their labors. They are not to talk against their masters to others. They are to be faithful not only outwardly but from the heart. They are not to be rebellious but are to recognize their proper place. The institution of slavery is not to be overthrown by means of their resistance and revolution, but it will be accomplished by means of the gospel. The King of peace overturns the evils by being peaceful!

Neither are the slaves to steal from their masters. This had become such a common practice among slaves so that the habit was no longer considered to be evil among them. The Christian slave is to have a greater sensitivity. He must be faithful in all things.

The manner of life which the Apostle holds before the slaves of that day will enable them to adorn the doctrine of God our Savior. These slaves who did not believe that they had any value or that they could contribute anything save their slave-labor are now told that theirs is the position of being able to "adorn" the doctrine revealed by God. If they live their confession they will be instrumental in showing the beauty of the gospel of Christ to others. Their attitude is of the greatest importance to the happiness and well-functioning of the family and even for the evaluation of the gospel by others. Their proper manner of life will do more for the destruction of the institution of slavery than any other method.

Questions for discussion:
1. Why is the Christian family so important? Can you have a strong society, church or nation without it?
2. What can the younger members learn from the older ones?
3. Do you think the Bible assigns an inferior role to the woman? What is the right or wrong about the idea of "women's liberation" today?
4. Is a home (or family) without children complete?
5. Is it "fair" to expect a minister's life to be an example to others?
6. Does the Bible condone slavery?

Lesson 14

Our Responsibility to the Gospel

Titus 2:11-15

All the things said about the family in the previous verses immediately recommend themselves for our approval. Indeed, if these principles are followed, the family will prosper. Yet, granted that these principles should be followed, how do we achieve this type of family relationship?

Applies to all of life

The Apostle Paul, following his great teacher, Jesus Christ, does not limit salvation to the benefits bestowed on the soul, but teaches that the salvation revealed in the gospel is very broad. It is a salvation which touches every part of human existence. Christ spoke of many subjects. He proclaimed the gospel of the kingdom! Paul preaches the same gospel and that gospel doesn't leave any part of life the same as it was before.

Paul has given his directions concerning the family. These are the things which are to be observed because the grace of God has appeared. God has sent His Son in the flesh and that has changed every part of life. Certainly, He has thereby given salvation in the narrow sense and has given the promise of eternal life, but, no part of life will ever be the same now that Christ has appeared.

The coming of Jesus Christ is the grace of God in its fullest depth. All the other blessings we receive in His grace find their origin in the coming of Jesus Christ in the flesh. This is the greatest event. That grace has *appeared*. It shone forth. The sun of righteousness was to arise, according to the prophet, to dispel the gloom of night. Sin had caused the night to descend on man. There was revelation in the Old Testament but it was still far from noonday light. Now that grace has appeared. No wonder that the people who were in darkness, seeing that great light arise, exclaimed that His name is: Wonderful!

Salvation for all classes

The great light which arose with the coming of Jesus Christ into this world penetrates into every part of life. Sin left no part of human life untouched and the light of the gospel doesn't either. When that grace of God appeared, it brought salvation to all men. No, Paul is not teaching a universalism. He never does. He has just spoken of various classes of people: aged men and aged women, younger men and women, parents and children, masters and servants.

The grace of God which is now revealed brings salvation to all these classes. No one need worry that his station in life does not qualify him for this salvation. Especially to the slaves this was an important message.

Instruction for sanctification

Now that grace of God which brings salvation to all men gives us instruction. It is an instruction which may not be limited to the instruction which a teacher gives to a pupil, although this is included. It is rather the *nurture* of which he speaks. This nurture includes the moral and spiritual as well as the intellectual part of man. This is that sanctification of which we speak. The grace of God remolds the whole man according to the pattern of Jesus Christ. That grace permeates every part of life. Sanctification is never completed in this life but it must begin to make its impact felt in every part of life. We are saved by grace; and here is an indication of what it means to be saved!

Our Responsibility to the Gospel

The instruction given us by this grace of God causes us to deny ungodliness and worldly lusts. It is a conscious rejection of idolatry and immorality. This is the negative aspect. We are also to live soberly and righteously and godly in this present world. We are to have self-discipline. We are to be fair in dealing with our neighbor. We are to be filled with devotion to God. This is the positive aspect of our sanctification. The old man of sin is to be put to death and the new man is to be quickened. When that process of sanctification progresses we begin to live according to both tables of the law of God. This is the way in which the life of the child of God must come to manifestation in this present time. The gospel brings responsibilities.

The coming of Jesus Christ in the flesh has brought an immeasurable joy to the heart of every believer. His faith now has an anchor. All the strands are brought together in the Christ. He is the fulfillment of all prophecy and ceremony. The love which God has revealed in sending His son and the love which the Son revealed by His obedience amazes every believer. Never have faith and love been revealed in such a way. That is the gospel — the good news now made known to men that the grace of God, which brings salvation to men, has appeared.

Looking forward

Glorious as this gospel is, there is still more. Hopes have indeed been revived by the coming of Jesus Christ in Bethlehem, but these hopes have not yet been fulfilled. We are therefore, says the Apostle, not only to look on the work accomplished by Jesus while He was here, but we are to look ahead to His coming again. He speaks of "the blessed hope." The believer is to look forward to the time when his faith shall become sight. He is to look forward to the time when his salvation is completed.

That will be a glorious appearing when Christ comes

again. His first coming was in humble surroundings and in impoverished conditions. When He comes again it will be in blinding glory. That too will be an "appearing." It will again be as the sun arises. This will be the appearing of "the great God and our Savior Jesus Christ." Both names refer to the same person. Our Savior, Who revealed Himself to His people in all His love and compassion, will then also be clearly manifested as "the great God." His deity was claimed and confessed while He was here in the flesh, but it was hidden. It will then be clear to all that He is God.

The gospel which is to be preached to the whole world is indeed rooted in the first coming of Christ. What a wealth is given to man in that gospel. However, it must include more. Man needs more. These are the things Jesus began to do... *I go to prepare a place for you.* We are to look forward to the time when He comes again when His work is completed. The believer is always to live in the *tension* between His first and second coming. The two are to be kept in balance. Only the true understanding of the first coming gives the proper view of the second coming. Properly viewed, it is a "blessed hope."

Zealous of good works

The One who is returning in great glory in the future is the same One who came in our flesh. While He was here in the flesh He gave Himself up for us as a sacrifice. He was the *Substitute* — He took the punishment which His people deserved. Only in this way was He able to redeem us, i.e., buy us back. He bought us free by the sacrifice of His own life. Iniquity would have slain us, but He paid the price so completely, that there wasn't a mite to be paid by the believer. Therefore they now belong to Him completely because He bought them. They are His possession. Not only has He engaged in this work to free us from the bonds of sin, but He has also purified His people by means of the

Our Responsibility to the Gospel

working of the Spirit within them. Not only are they set free but they are also renewed. Not only does He justify, He also sanctifies. Because of that they are now become zealous of good works. Good works done out of gratitude? — Yes, but the spirit of gratitude must also be given His people.

This is the gospel which Titus must teach. This is the gospel which is complete. This is the gospel which does not end with the works of God done in the past, but also stretches out to those things which are still future. Paul does not speak of the second coming of Christ all the time to the exclusion of the things revealed in the first coming. He keeps the proper balance. At the same time, this is the full, the complete gospel — and anything less is no gospel. Titus must preach this gospel. He must preach election and human responsibility; first coming of Christ and second coming; justification and sanctification. Then the whole counsel of God will be proclaimed.

Keep on preaching

Titus must keep on preaching these things. This must not be done in a cold manner, but he must be urgent in his message. It may be necessary to admonish men concerning these matters. The message must be brought as coming from the heart of God! Do this with all authority, says Paul. God sends His ambassadors (of whom Titus is one) and they are to speak in the name of the King.

Let it be made clear to all that the gospel is not just another philosophy which presents itself to the judgment of men, but that it is the King's command. The last statement of this chapter agrees with this. Let no man despise (or ignore) thee. To ignore the word of the ambassador is the greatest insult imaginable to the King in whose name he speaks. Don't let that happen! But, how are you going to prevent it? By making it abundantly clear that you are not bringing your own word but the word of Another. By making it clear that you are not an errand boy but indeed, an ambassador of the King. Paul magnifies his office — so should Titus.

Questions for discussion:
1. How does the grace of God which has brought salvation change everything? What is salvation? Does one's personality also need salvation?
2. What is the difference between justification and sanctification? Are we to be active in either one?
3. What do you think of those who are always talking about the second coming? Do we speak enough about this subject? Do we have to know the whole order of events at the end of time to be able to look forward to it?
4. How important is the substitutionary atonement?
5. Is Paul's view of office sufficiently clarified in only those passages which speak specifically about the nature and duties of office?

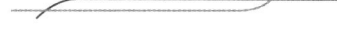

Lesson 15

Attitude Toward Non-Christians

Titus 3:1-7

At the time when Paul was writing his various epistles, the churches were small and the membership consisted of a very small percentage of the population. How would these small groups be able to exist in a hostile world?

That of course, has always been a problem for the church. Humanly speaking the church would be swallowed up by the world. Her continued existence is a clear indication of her *origin*. Yet, she may not have the attitude: The church is Christ's and therefore it makes no difference how she conducts herself — her continuation is assured. No, the Apostle here gives instructions to Titus concerning the deportment of the members of the church toward those who are without.

Subjection to rulers

First of all Titus must remind the members of the church that they are to be in subjection to rulers and authorities. Time and again he refers to this matter in his writings. What is the reason for this? The Jews, who had their own land and government so many years, found it very difficult to render obedience to Roman authorities. The people on the island of Crete shared a similar contempt for Roman rule.

The church of Jesus Christ must set a good example. The people of the church bow before the fifth commandment. They are not merely to show outward obedience, but they are to render willing obedience. The government should realize that the church of Christ is its greatest supporter.

This is the duty of the people of God and Titus must remind them of this.

Showing meekness toward all

The believer must not speak evil of his unbelieving neighbors even though there seems to be reason enough (1:12). He must bridle his tongue. Speaking evil of his fellowman will only alienate him more.

The believer must not be contentious, i.e., he must not have a desire to fight. He must be gentle — ready to sacrifice personal gain for the sake of others. Ready to give help — to be reasonable. Besides this he must show all meekness to *all* men. Many of the people on Crete were not reasonable or likeable but the Christian is to show a mild temperament toward all men. Not only to the loveable but also to those who are difficult. What an assignment! How can anyone do these things?

A reasonable assignment

First the Apostle shows Titus and the church to which he ministers that this is indeed a reasonable assignment. He reminds them that they were formerly the same kind of people as the unbelievers surrounding them now. He includes himself and Titus among those who were far removed from the ideal. They also had once been without understanding of even the basic things of the gospel. They also had once been disobedient to all authority. They were formerly deceived into believing they were free while they were the slaves of their own lusts and pleasures. They lived a life of malice and envy. They had been hateful, offensive, detestable. Thus they hated one another.

What a catalog of evils! Yet, these things must be borne in mind so that you will have pity on those who are still living that kind of life. You will not be so impatient with these people if you remember that you lived the same kind of life not long ago.

Attitude Toward Non-Christians

Salvation makes the difference

But, though it may be well to be reminded of their former manner of life, that, in itself, will not enable anyone to do those things of which Paul has spoken in the first two verses of this chapter. More is needed — and much more is now given! Salvation alone prepares to every good work.

The next four verses form one sentence. The one thought crowds in upon the other. This is typically Pauline! The life which they lived in former days was indeed a sad one." But when the kindness of God... appeared!" That made all the difference. One could have spoken to them every day concerning the things they ought to do, but it would make no difference. Man is not able to do these things by himself. But, God intervened. His kindness and love to man *appeared! That* was the coming of Jesus Christ in the flesh. There a love and a kindness was shown as the world had never seen it before.

The heart of the whole matter is found in verse 5 where the Apostle says that He saved us. This salvation has not only rescued man from perdition, but it has also changed his whole life here and now. It has changed man's whole relation to his fellowman. It has changed his whole personality. The things which were impossible for him in former times have now become possible. He saved us; and, therefore, nothing is the same. When the heart of this passage has been clearly seen, we will not find the modifying phrases and clauses too difficult.

God's kindness and love have been shown us in the salvation He has revealed. This salvation was not obtained by our works but by His mercy. The author speaks of works done by us in a state of righteousness — as though there were such a state! He emphasizes the fact that the works which we did ourselves are of no benefit for salvation. Our works are not the *ground* of our salvation, but he would see these works now as the *fruit* of our salvation! He saved us. It is His work from beginning to end. It was done according to His mercy. We were those who were in need of mercy — benevolence. The need must be realized and admitted in order to obtain the mercy of God.

We were not saved by our own works, no, God saved us in His mercy. How was that salvation accomplished? He regenerated and renewed us by His Spirit. By nature man was dead spiritually (Eph. 2:1). That is the simple way in which Paul speaks of man's total depravity. For such as are dead in sins the first need is to be made alive. That is regeneration! The life-giving Spirit of God has made man alive again and so he is renewed in all of life. Paul speaks here of the "washing of regeneration" whereby he makes reference to baptism. He does not say that baptism regenerates — that is the work of the Spirit and not of a sacrament. The best explanation, it seems to me, is this: baptism is the sacrament of regeneration. Therefore the "washing" and the "regeneration" are spoken of in the same breath.

Renewing of the Holy Spirit

The Spirit of God has been poured out richly on the people of God. Here the Apostle is referring to Pentecost. The outpouring of the Spirit on that day has changed everything for believers. Before that time His people also enjoyed the indwelling of the Spirit (Ps. 51:11) but He is now given in far greater measure. The New Testament people of God are favored far above those of the old Testament times. Pentecost was the direct result of the accomplished salvation by Jesus Christ. He promised His disciples that He would send the Spirit so that they would be enriched far more than by His (Jesus) physical presence with them.

He saved us. This thought is so rich, no one, not even an Apostle, can exhaust its meaning. It is the heart of the

Attitude Toward Non-Christians

gospel. We could never have worked it out ourselves. The kindness, love and mercy of God are therein brought to light. Jesus Christ is our Savior. He has sent His Holy Spirit to give new life and to renew. The gift has been given us in abundant measure.

But, there is still more! We are now justified by His grace. God, the Judge, declares us innocent. Our sins are no more! The perfect righteousness of Jesus Christ is now credited to us! That is grace! That is not merited by us. That is true salvation. We know what the verdict will be when we stand before the judgment seat of the Judge of all the earth — Innocent! Judgment day has been turned into Victory Day for the people of God. Salvation is complete. No one shall lay anything to the charge of God's elect (Rom. 8:33).

An ongoing struggle

Although the salvation of God's people has been completed through the work of Jesus Christ so that nothing need nor can be added to it, we are not yet in possession of that completed salvation. His people must still struggle against indwelling sin. They are, therefore, heirs of eternal life. They live in hope, but, it is a hope which will surely be fulfilled. They are heirs, i.e., those not yet in possession of the full wealth, but, those who will certainly receive it when the proper time has arrived. They are heirs of "eternal life," i.e., the true life which will never end.

Because all these gifts are theirs, the Christians on Crete must live according to the instructions of the first two verses of this chapter. It has been made possible through the salvation they have received. This salvation renews the whole person. Indeed, the gospel speaks to every area of life; and it also speaks to every part of an individual's person.

II Timothy & Titus

Questions for discussion:
1. Why does the doctrine of good works seem to be so difficult for Reformed people? Is there good reason why the Heidelberg Catechism treats this matter no less than three different times?
2. How do you explain this seeming contradiction: We are to do good works to win others for Christ (H. Cat. Q. 86) while only the elect are saved?
3. What does regeneration or being born again mean? Are there any Christians other than those who are born again?
4. What is the difference between justification and sanctification?
5. What is your evaluation of the slogan: *Jesus saves*, in the light of the verses 4-7 of this chapter?

Lesson 16

Final Instructions and Greetings

Titus 3:8-15

The Pastoral Epistles are brief and in them one does not find the longer development of various doctrines as are found in the earlier epistles of Paul. Here everything moves at a rapid pace.

A faithful saying

Once more Paul makes mention of a "faithful saying." This is the fifth such saying. Each one of them refers to those things concerning which there can be no debate. Each "saying" expresses that which the church confesses and has received the status of an early "Confession" or creed.

By this particular saying Paul refers to those things which he has written in the previous verses. There can be no doubt about the manifestation of salvation as there described. That salvation was wrought by the Triune God. It is not dependent on our works. These things must be emphasized by Titus. He must affirm these things confidently. The heart of the gospel must be proclaimed again and again and it must be done in such a way that it leaves no reason for anyone to doubt it. Only in this way will it give assurance to those who hear and believe the gospel.

When such assurance is found in the hearts of believers, they will do the good works which the gospel demands. Only a strong faith will lead to the desired action. One could emphasize the doing of the deed endlessly but the desired results would not appear. Only the wholehearted acceptance of the gospel will produce those works which are required. Then they will desire to do such works.

They will then live their faith! This is good and profitable.

Shun vain teachings

If Titus will emphasize the heart of the gospel of God it will become clear to him that he is not to waste his time refuting the unprofitable and vain teachings of other so-called teachers. In his letters to Timothy, Paul had also given warning concerning some of these teachers. They engage in foolish questionings. They mislead people by finding various teachings or "lessons" in the genealogies which are not there. These genealogies were given for a purpose and were by no means foolish additions to the revelation! However, their purpose was to show the relationship of the one generation to the other and the continuity of the promise and faithfulness of their God. One must not look for more. It is a real temptation for some to find special meaning in numbers or names while *usually* numbers are only used for specifics and exactness and names are *usually* used only to distinguish one person from another!

Titus is also warned about those who strive and fight about the law. All kinds of hidden meanings were sought regarding the various commandments. Of course that leads to strife! No one has a standard whereby he can measure his "interpretation;" and, as a result, the view of the one is as good (or bad) as the other! This kind of teaching is not profitable for any person and will surely not build up the church in faith. Such teachings are vain, empty. Titus must shun such debates.

Reject heretics

While there are those whom Titus must shun, there are others whom he must "refuse" or reject because they are far more dangerous. These are heretics, people who come with a different doctrine than that of the gospel of Christ.

Final Instructions and Greetings

Such people are "perverted" — they do not think straight. They are seeking to introduce a substitute gospel. This is sin. Such a person has heard the gospel and refuses it, and places something else in its place. Such people are self-condemned, i.e., they know better and still continue in their evil way. They sin against their own conscience. But, they are not only committing sins themselves, they also endanger the church. They may lead others astray. Therefore Titus must assume a different attitude toward these than to those of whom the Apostle spoke before. These must be rejected.

Yet, although these teachings must be rejected and also the persons who are spreading these heresies must be rejected, this is not to be done in a casual manner. Paul speaks of a first and second admonition. Such a person must be admonished *officially*. He must be admonished on the authority of the church! This is more than a private conversation! The evil of his way must be pointed out to him very clearly. If the first admonition does not lead to repentance, admonish him again. The Apostle is here emphasizing the basic elements of church discipline. It is not enough to confront the sinner with the error of his way. There is too much at stake. The church is to be patient. If at all possible the sinner must be rescued. However, if both the first and second admonitions meet with stubborn resistance, he must be rejected because the body of Christ, the church, is more important than any individual. The Apostle counsels Titus to be patient in love but also to be firm.

Titus requested to come

Paul is coming to the end of his epistle. He has dealt briefly with some of the most important problems Titus has to face. Further instructions can be given later.

Paul now tells Titus to do everything possible to come to visit him in Nicopolis where he intends to spend the winter. Winter traveling, especially by ship, was very dangerous at this time. No doubt, Paul will have many things to do even though he will be restricted somewhat during the winter season. Titus should come to him. He urges this, but does not say why he should come. The epistle has been brief. There will be many things to consider and talk about when they meet face to face.

There is also a longing of Paul to see his co-worker in the gospel. He wants to see Timothy while he is imprisoned. Now he wants to see Titus. However, even though the desire to visit with Titus is strong, the church on Crete must not suffer for it. It is not the kind of church which can stand to be "vacant" for a period of time. The coming of Titus is, therefore, contingent on the availability of Artemas or Tychicus. One of them must be able to take over for Titus in his absence. The church always comes first with Paul. We know nothing of Artemas and little of Tychicus. However, they were trusted men — well-qualified to care for the church on Crete while Titus was absent.

Provide for Christ's ambassadors

Paul is sending this letter to Titus by the hand of Zenas and Apollos. Zenas is a lawyer and may be able to help Titus in his battle with those who are striving and fighting about the law. Apollos is the famed orator. The people of the church on Crete should be happy to have him fill the pulpit there while he is visiting Titus.

But, when these men arrive, they should be well cared for. Evidently these men had to travel farther. They are to be provided with food and lodging while they are on the island of Crete and must then also be given those things which are needed to continue their journey.

The burden and responsibility for the care of these ambassadors should not fall only on the "minister" of the church of Crete,but the members of the congregation should learn to do their duty regarding these matters. They should

Final Instructions and Greetings

learn to apply themselves to good works. The care for these "ambassadors" certainly belongs to the "necessary uses." The church here has received much — it is now time for the fruits to appear! These will be the fruits of the gospel or the fruits of faith. These fruits are not required for doing something great, but for the very common tasks of giving food and lodging to ambassadors of Christ. So must fruit-bearing begin.

Salutations and benediction

"All that are with me salute thee" — but we don't know who were with Paul at this time. Sometimes he refers to others who are with him in the beginning of his letters, but not in this one. It is foolish to speculate as to the people who are meant when he doesn't tell us. Titus, however, must have known who they were or this statement would be meaningless.

Titus is also to bring the Apostolic greeting to "them that love us in faith," that is, the faithful and believing people in the church on Crete. Paul has such a warm spot in his heart for all those who confess a common faith with him. That bond of faith is very strong. It is even stronger than the body of blood. This man loves Christ and consequently loves His people.

"Grace be with you all." That is the brief Apostolic blessing. At times Paul gives a longer benediction. However, he doesn't have to spell it out to Titus. It is the grace. That is the grace of God which contains all that is necessary for any believer.

Questions for discussion:
1. Is there a danger that the "Positive Preaching" to which vs. 8 refers will bring forth only the old things and not the new? Explain.

II Timothy & Titus

2. Is there a danger that people will always be told what to do without giving them the basis on which they should do things?
3. Do you think Hebrew parents were able to give meaningful names to their children more than we? Cf. Luke 1:59-61.
4. Is there greater danger of being too patient in discipline or not patient enough today? What standard should be followed?
5. Is it a more appealing fruit of faith to do something spectacular with our support than to take care of necessary local things?

Notes